Bette Midler; James L. Nederlander; Garry McQuinn; Liz Koops; Michael Hamlyn; Allan Scott; Roy Furman/Richard Willis;

Terry Allen Kramer; Terri and Timothy Childs, Ken Greiner, Ruth Hendel; Chugg Entertainment; Michael Buckley;

Stewart F. Lane/Bonnie Comley; Bruce Davey; Thierry Suc /TS3; Bartner/Jenkins; Broadway Across America/H. Koenigsberg;

M. Lerner/D. Bisno/K. Seidel/R. Gold; Paul Boskind and Martian Entertainment/Spirtas-Mauro Productions/MAS Music Arts & Show; and David Mirvish

In association with **MGM ON STAGE**
Darcie Denkert and Dean Stolber
Present

PRISCILLA
QUEEN OF THE DESERT
the musical

Book by
STEPHAN ELLIOTT & ALLAN SCOTT
Based on the Latent Image/ Specific Films Motion Picture
Distributed by Metro-Goldwyn-Mayer Inc.

Starring

WILL SWENSON	TONY SHELDON	NICK ADAMS	C. DAVID JOHNSON

with

JAMES BROWN III   NATHAN LEE GRAHAM   J. ELAINE MARCOS   MIKE MCGOWAN   JESSICA PHILLIPS   STEVE SCHEPIS   KEALA SETTLE

and

JACQUELINE B. ARNOLD   ANASTACIA MCCLESKEY   ASHLEY SPENCER

THOM ALLISON   KYLE BROWN   JOSHUA BUSCHER   GAVIN LODGE   LUKE MANNIKUS   ELLYN MARIE MARSH   JEFF METZLER
ERIC SCIOTTO   AMAKER SMITH   ESTHER STILWELL   BRYAN WEST   TAD WILSON   ASHTON WOERZ

Bus Concept & Production Design BRIAN THOMSON	*Costume Design* TIM CHAPPEL & LIZZY GARDINER	*Lighting Design* NICK SCHLIEPER	*Sound Design* JONATHAN DEANS & PETER FITZGERALD
Orchestrations STEPHEN "SPUD" MURPHY & CHARLIE HULL	*Musical Coordinator* JOHN MILLER	*Music Director* JEFFREY KLITZ	*Developed for the Stage By* SIMON PHILLIPS
Casting TELSEY + COMPANY	*Press Representative* BONEAU/BRYAN-BROWN	*Advertising* SPOTCO	*Director of Marketing* NICK PRAMIK
Technical Supervisor DAVID BENKEN	*Production Stage Manager* DAVID HYSLOP	*Flying By* FOY	*Makeup Design* CASSIE HANLON

Associate Director DEAN BRYANT	*Associate Choreographer* ANDREW HALLSWORTH	*Associate Producer* KEN SUNSHINE

General Manager B.J. HOLT	*Executive Producer* ALECIA PARKER

Production Supervised by
JERRY MITCHELL

Music Supervision & Arrangements
STEPHEN "SPUD" MURPHY

Choreographer
ROSS COLEMAN

Director
SIMON PHILLIPS

The original motion picture was written by Stephan Elliott, produced by Al Clark and Michael Hamlyn, executive producer Rebel Penfold-Russell and was financed with the assistance of the Film Finance Corporation of Australia Limited and the New South Wales Film and Television Office.

Illustration by Maciej Hajnrich

ISBN 978-1-4584-1452-6

HAL•LEONARD®
CORPORATION
7777 W. BLUEMOUND RD. P.O.BOX 13819 MILWAUKEE, WI 53213

Visit Hal Leonard Online at
www.halleonard.com

IT'S RAINING MEN

Words and Music by PAUL JABARA
and PAUL SHAFFER

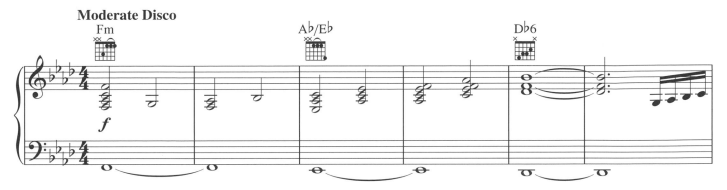

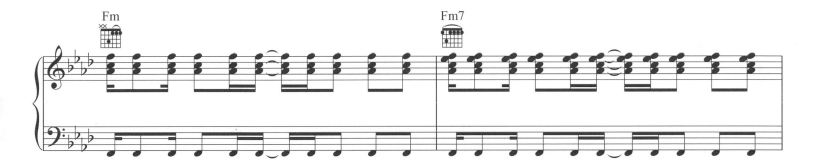

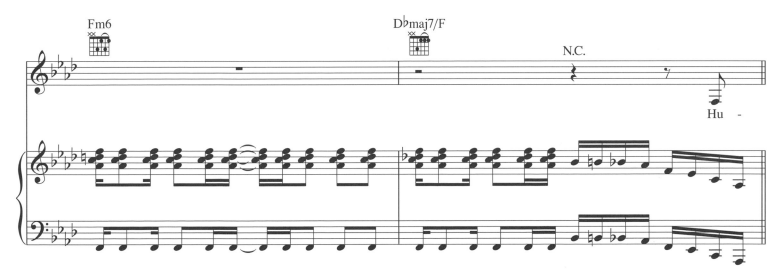

Hu -

mid - i - ty's ris - ing.   Ba -

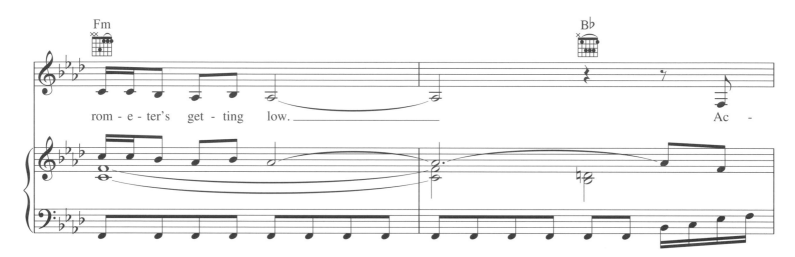

rom - e - ter's get - ting low. _____   Ac -

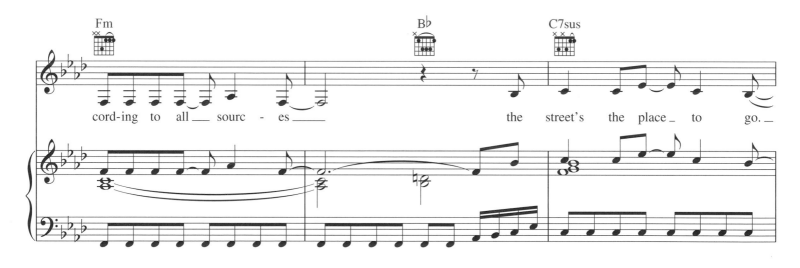

cord-ing to all __ sourc - es ___   the street's the place __ to go. __

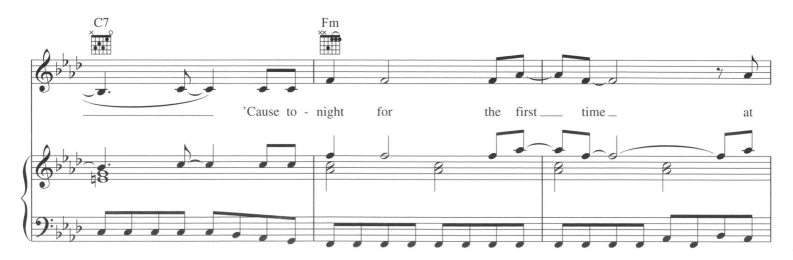

_____ 'Cause to - night for   the first __ time __   at

just a-bout half past ten, for the first time in his-

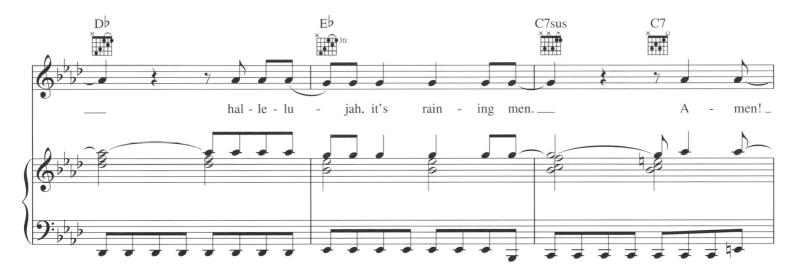

-to-ry it's gon-na start rain-ing men. It's rain-ing men,

hal-le-lu-jah, it's rain-ing men. A-men!

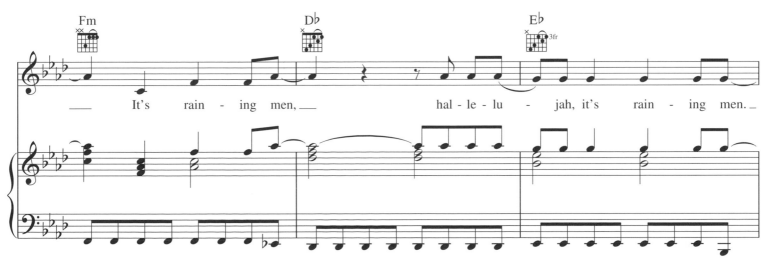

It's rain-ing men, hal-le-lu-jah, it's rain-ing men.

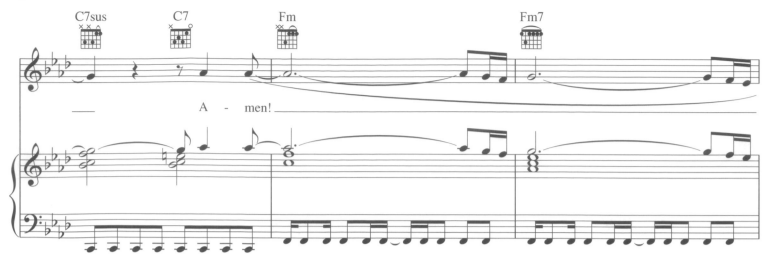

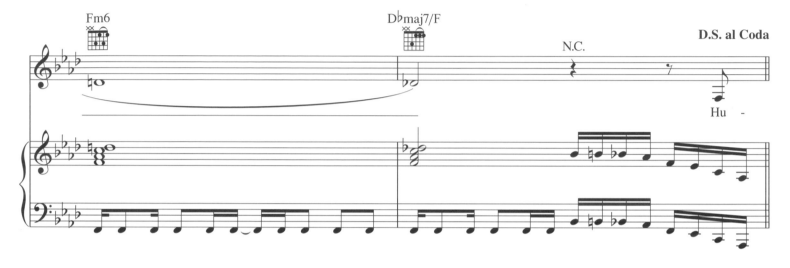

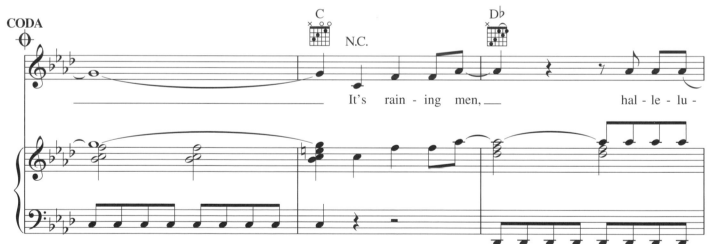

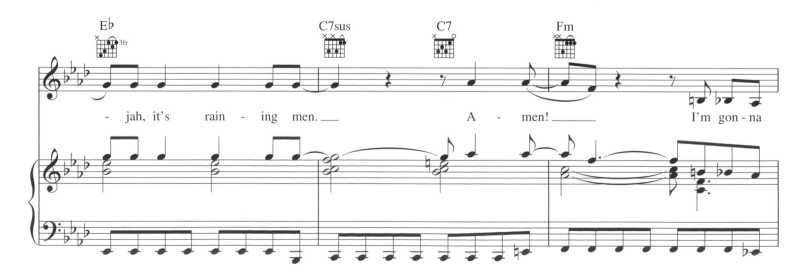

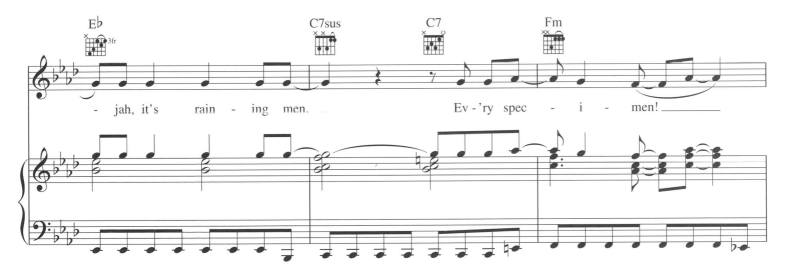

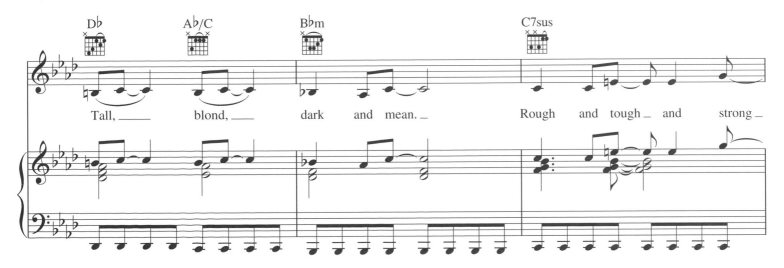

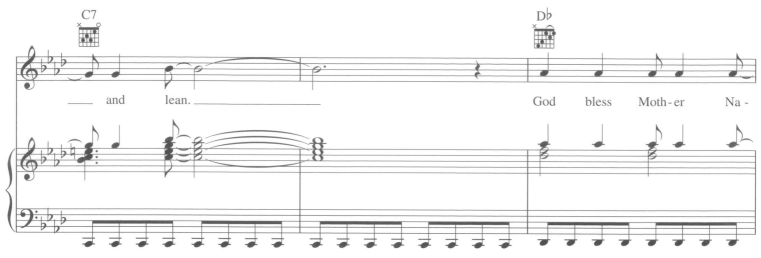

and lean. God bless Moth-er Na-

-ture. _ She's a sin-gle wom-an too. _

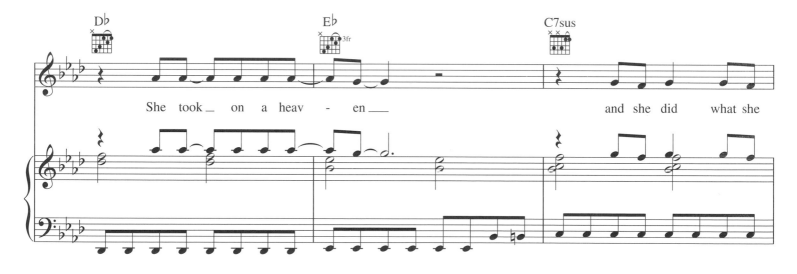

She took_ on a heav-en _ and she did what she

had to do. She taught_ ev-'ry an-gel _

to re-ar-range the sky ___ so that each and ev-'ry wom-

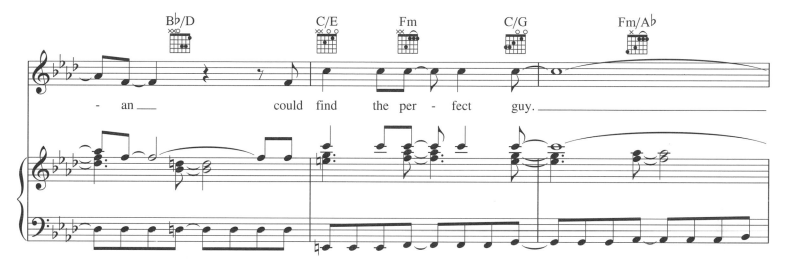

-an ___ could find the per-fect guy. ___

It's rain-ing men. ___

Spoken: Go get yourself wet, girl!

I know you want to.

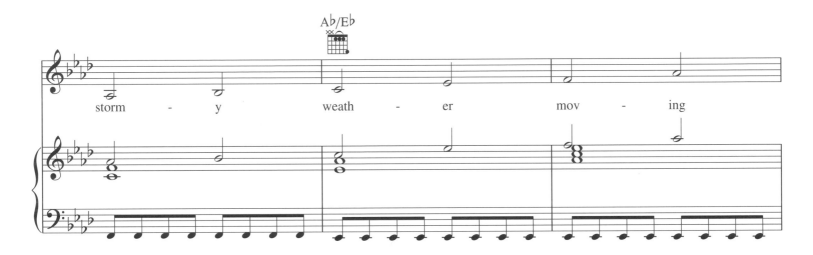

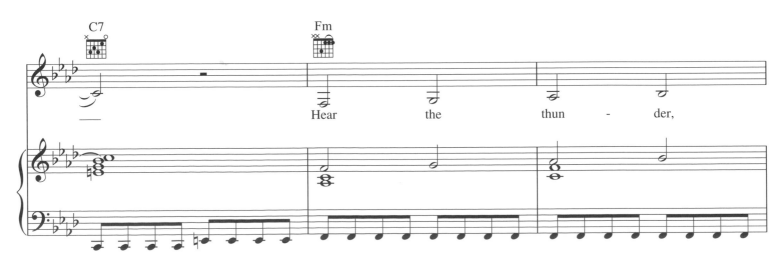

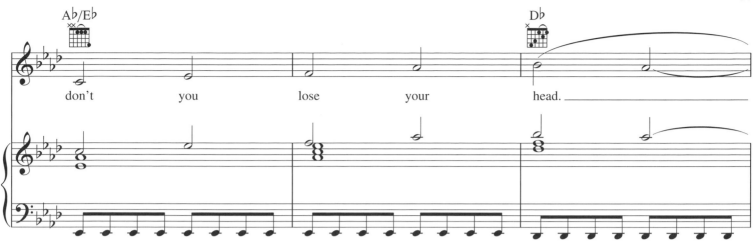

don't you lose your head. _____

_____ Rip off the roof _____ and stay _____ in bed. _____

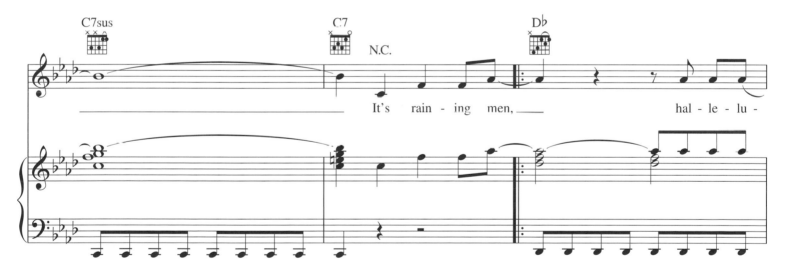

_____ It's rain - ing men, _____ hal - le - lu -

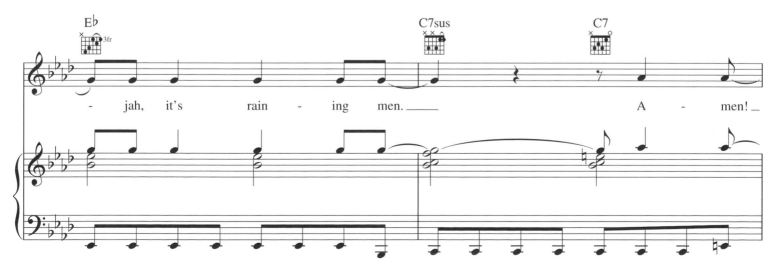

- jah, it's rain - ing men. _____ A - men! _____

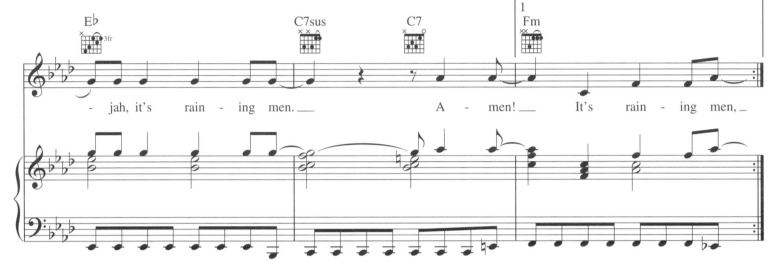

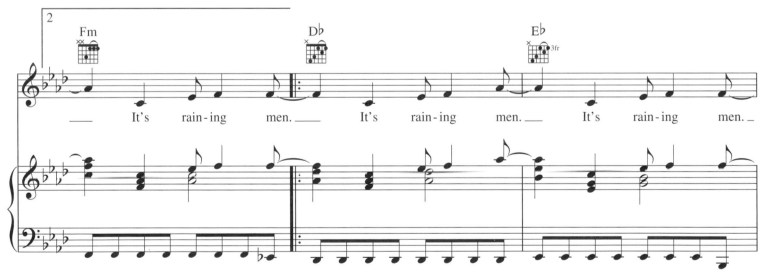

WHAT'S LOVE GOT TO DO WITH IT

Words and Music by TERRY BRITTEN
and GRAHAM LYLE

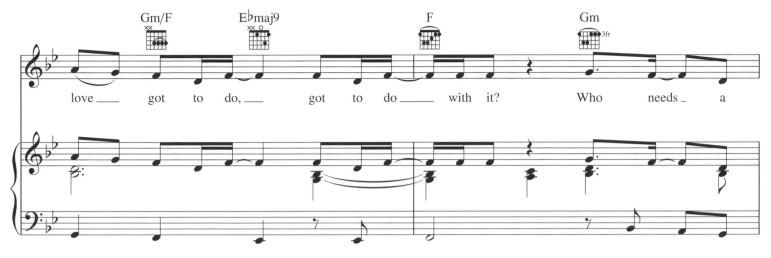

DON'T LEAVE ME THIS WAY

Words and Music by KENNETH GAMBLE,
LEON HUFF and CARY GILBERT

ba - by please. }
out your love. }
Don't leave me this way.
Ah. _____

Ba - by, my heart is full with love and de - sire for you. Now

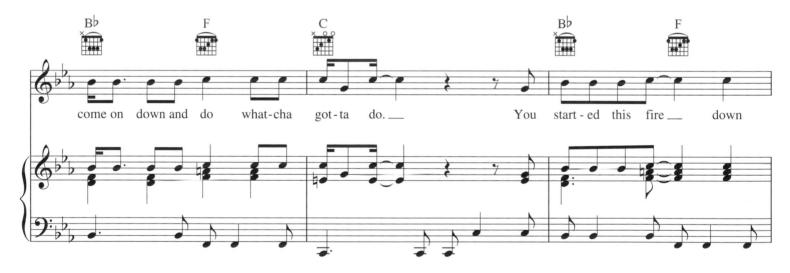

come on down and do what-cha got - ta do. ___ You start - ed this fire ___ down

in my soul. Now can't-cha see it's burn - in' out - ta con - trol.

Come on sat - is - fy the need in me ___ 'cause on - ly your ___ good lov - in' can

set me free. set me free.

Please.

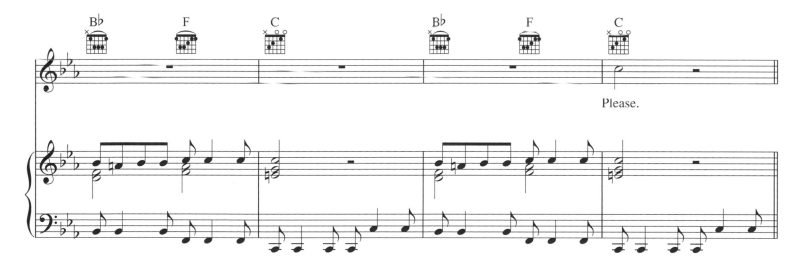

Please, please don't go. ___ Please, please don't go. ___

Repeat and Fade

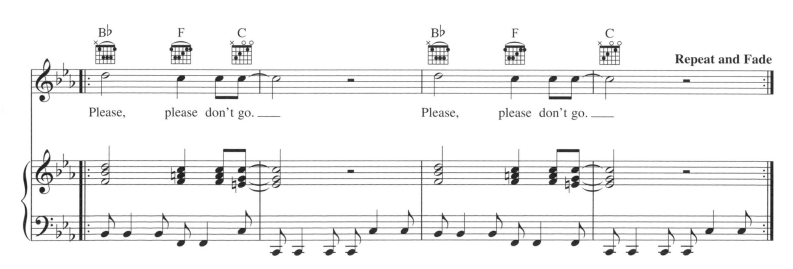

MATERIAL GIRL

Words and Music by PETER BROWN
and ROBERT RANS

Some boys kiss __ me, some __ boys hug __ me. I ____
Some boys ro - mance, some __ boys slow __ dance. That's __

__ think they're O. K. _____ If they don't give __ me prop -
__ all right with me. _____ If they can't raise __ my in -

- er cred - it, I _____ just walk __ a - way. _____
- t'rest then __ I have __ to let __ them be. _____

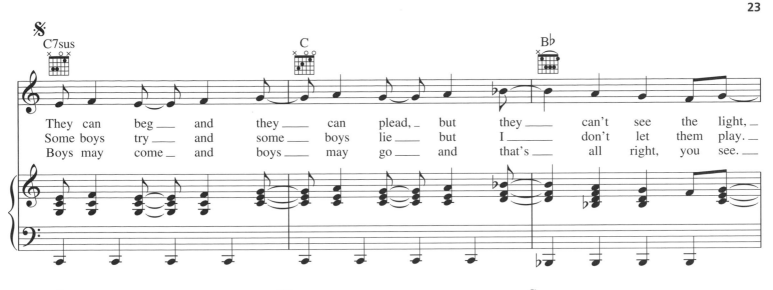

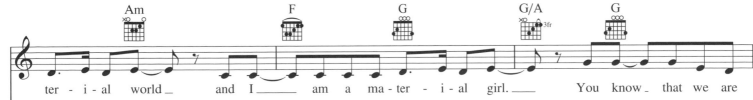

GO WEST

Words and Music by JACQUES MORALI,
HENRI BELOLO and VICTOR WILLIS

I SAY A LITTLE PRAYER

Lyric by HAL DAVID
Music by BURT BACHARACH

Moderately fast

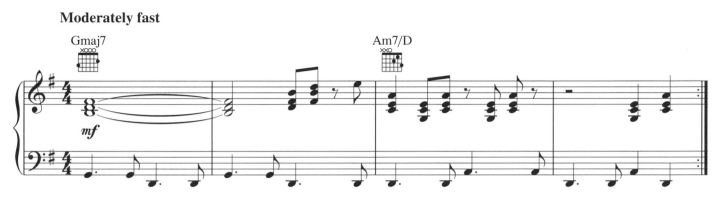

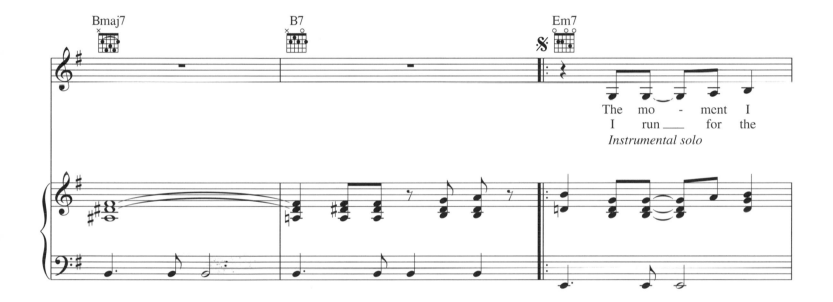

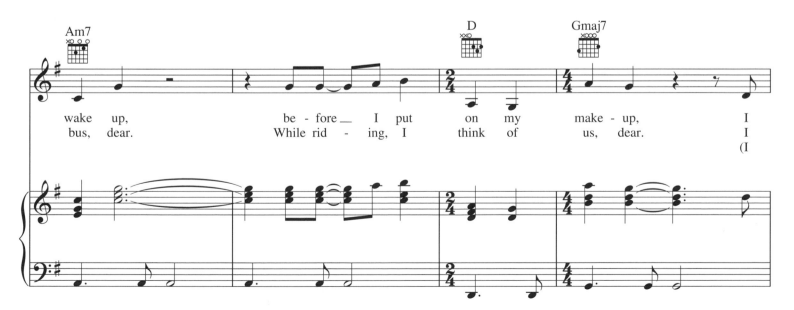

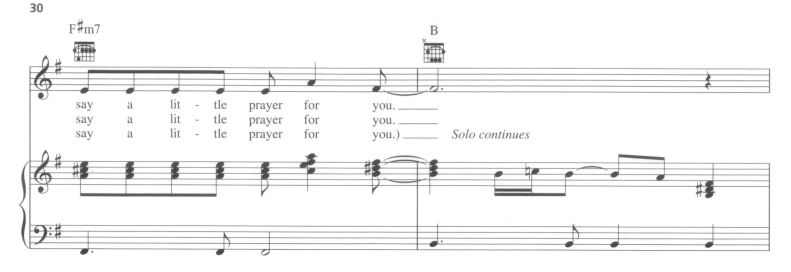

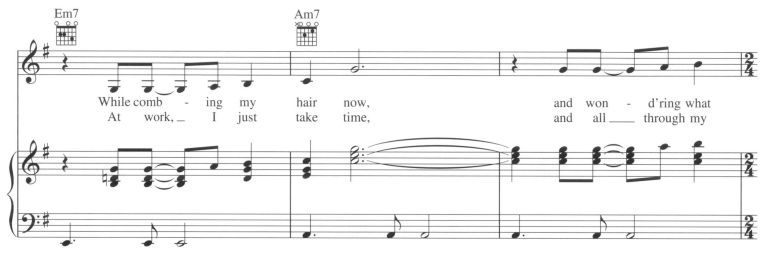

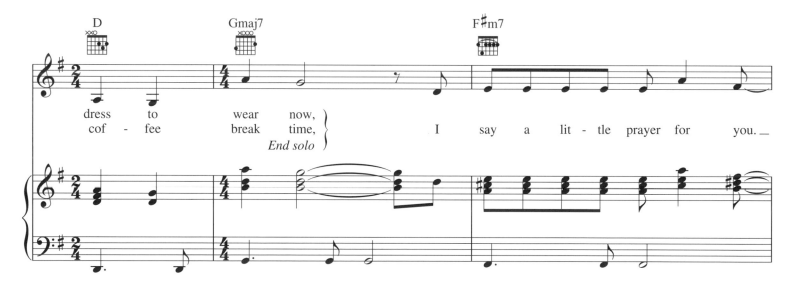

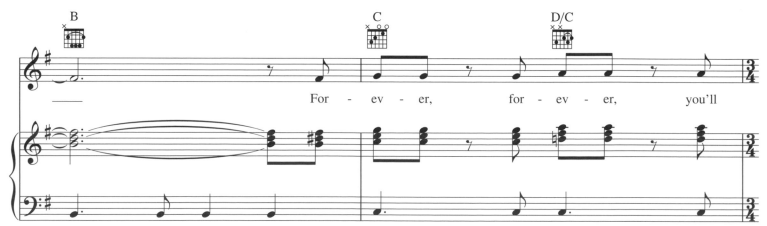

stay in my heart ___ and I will love you. For - ev - er and ev - er, we

nev - er will part. ___ Oh, how I'll love you. To - geth - er, to - geth - er, that's

how it must be. ___ To live with - out you would on - ly mean heart - break for

me. ___

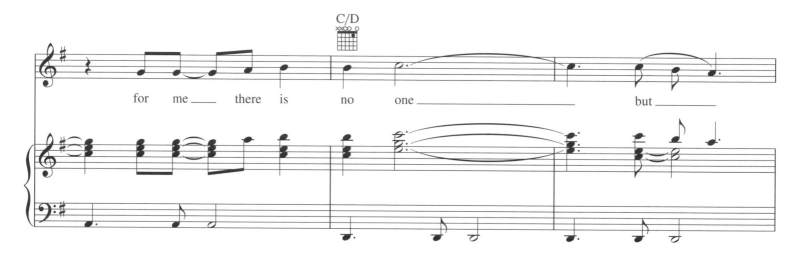

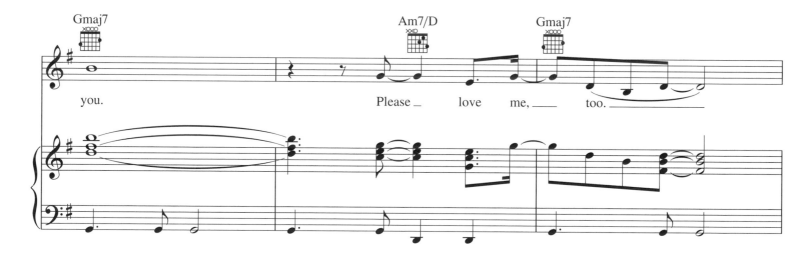

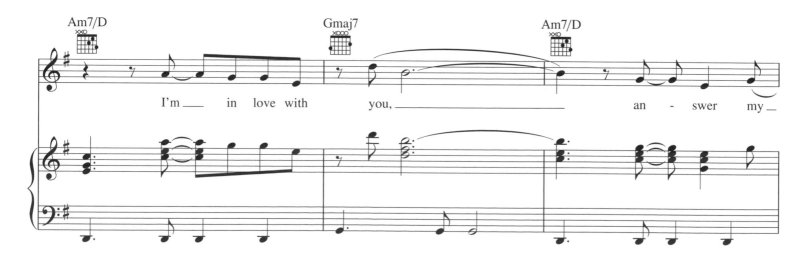

prayer. Say ___ you love me, too. ___

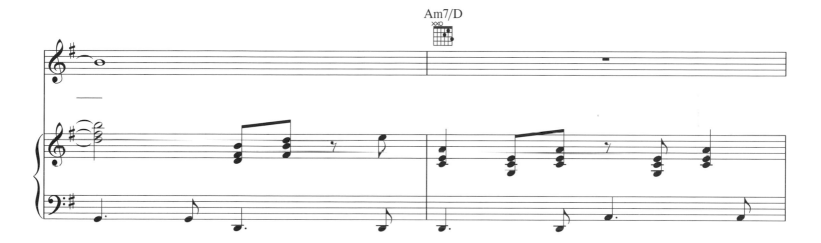

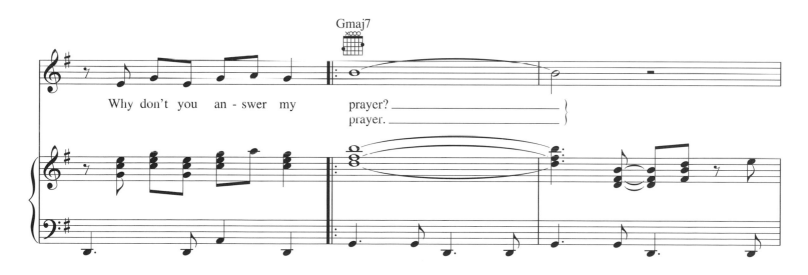

Why don't you an-swer my prayer? ___
prayer. ___

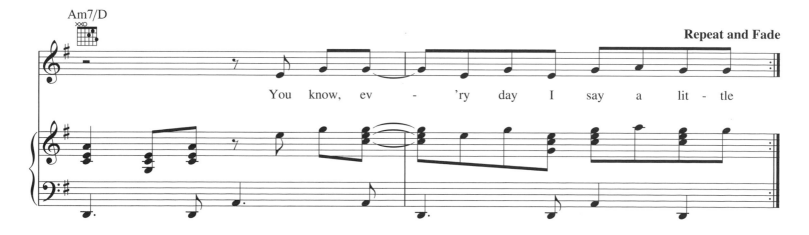

Repeat and Fade

You know, ev-'ry day I say a lit-tle

I LOVE THE NIGHT LIFE

Words and Music by ALICIA BRIDGES
and SUSAN HUTCHESON

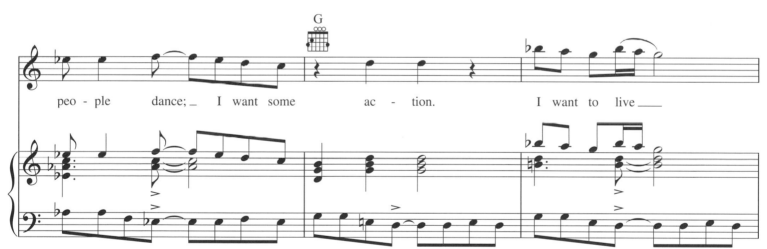

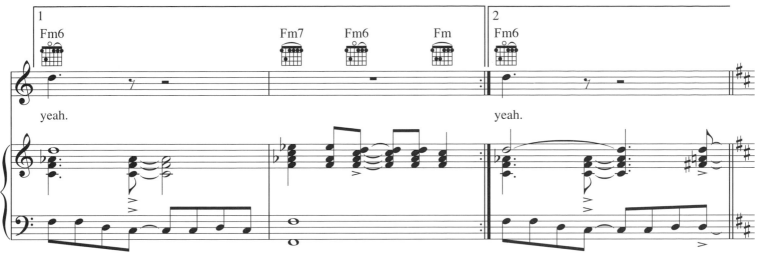

TRUE COLORS

Words and Music by BILLY STEINBERG
and TOM KELLY

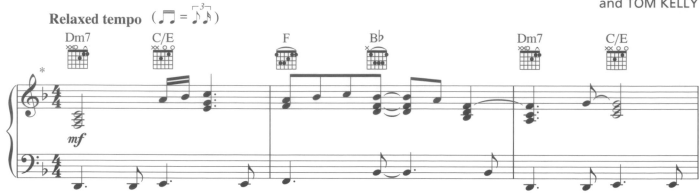

You with the

sad   eyes,   don't be dis-cour - aged. Oh, I re-al - ize   it's
smile   then,   don't be un-hap - py. Can't re-mem-ber when   I

hard   to take cour - age.   In   a world   full of peo - ple
last saw you laugh - ing.   If   this world makes you cra - zy   and you're

Recorded a half step higher.

true col - ors are beau - ti - ful, ooh, __ like a rain - bow.

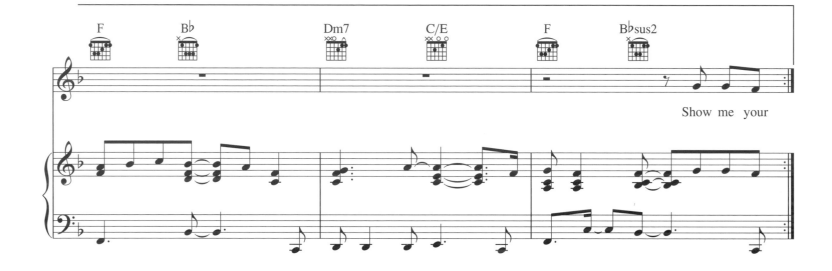

Show me your

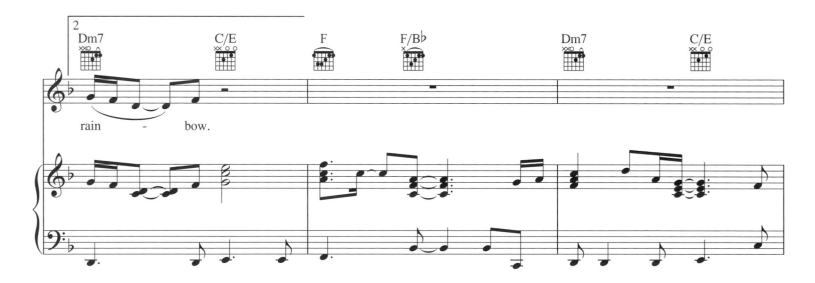

rain - bow.

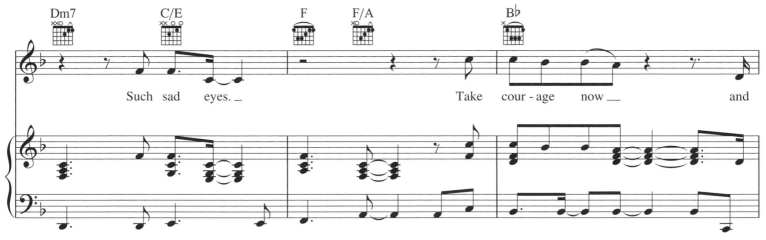

Such sad eyes. _ Take cour-age now _ and

re - al - ize, when this world makes you cra - zy and you're

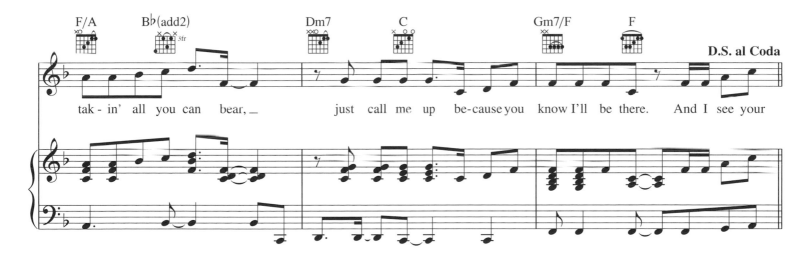

D.S. al Coda

tak - in' all you can bear, _ just call me up be-cause you know I'll be there. And I see your

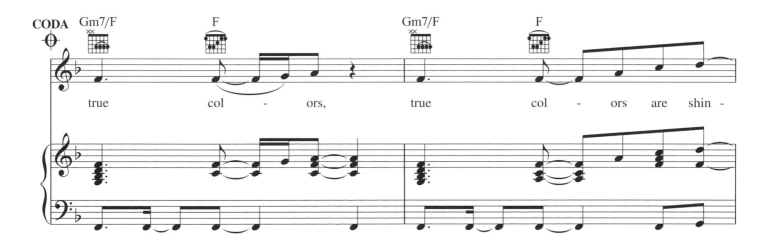

CODA

true col - ors, true col - ors are shin -

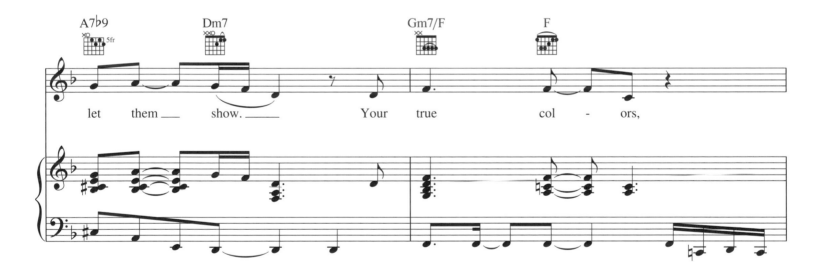

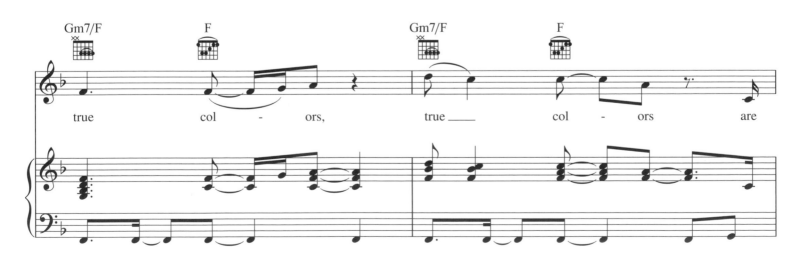

beau-ti-ful, beau-ti-ful like a rain - bow.

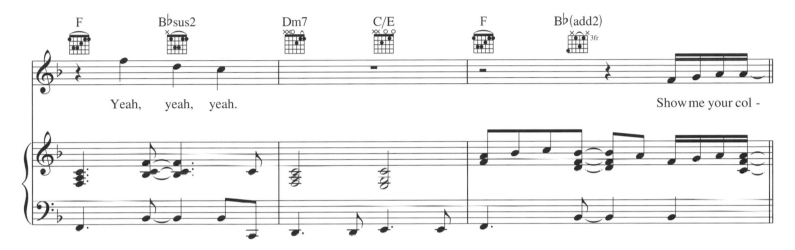

Yeah, yeah, yeah. Show me your col -

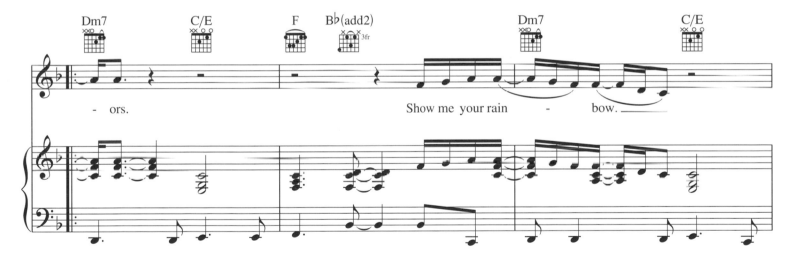

- ors. Show me your rain - bow. ___

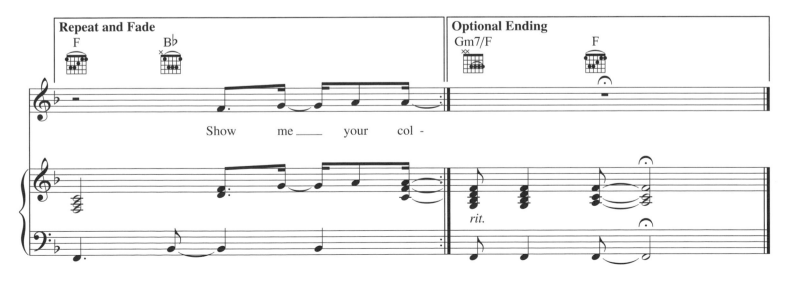

Repeat and Fade

Show me ___ your col -

Optional Ending

rit.

COLOR MY WORLD

Words and Music by JACKIE TRENT
and TONY HATCH

You'll nev-er see a dark cloud hang-ing round me, _____
Just as long as I know you're think-ing of me, _____

_____ now there is on-ly blue sky to sur-
_____ there'll be a rain-bow al-ways up a-

round me. _____ There's nev-er been a
bove me. _____ Since I _____ found the

Cm7/Bb

grey day since you found me. _____
one who real-ly loves me. _____

F7   Bb

Ev-'ry-thing I touch is turn-ing to gold. _____

Bb   Db   Eb

_____ So, you can col-or my world with sun-shine yel-low each

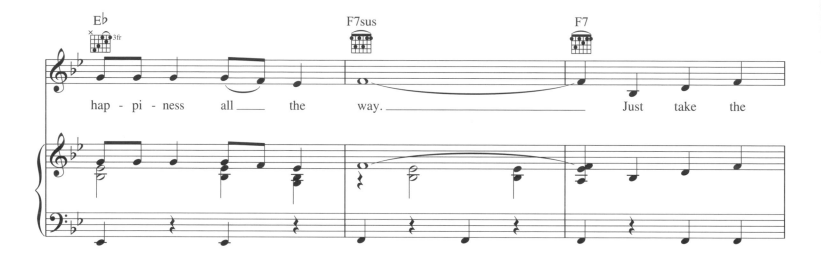

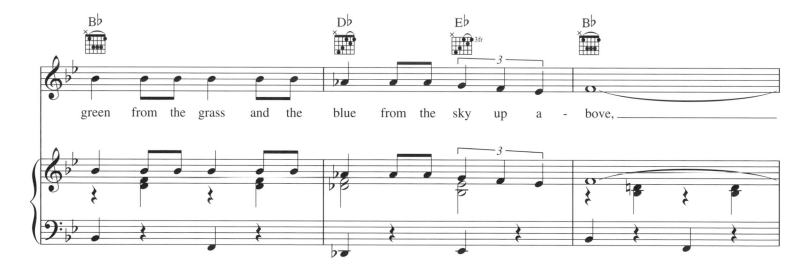

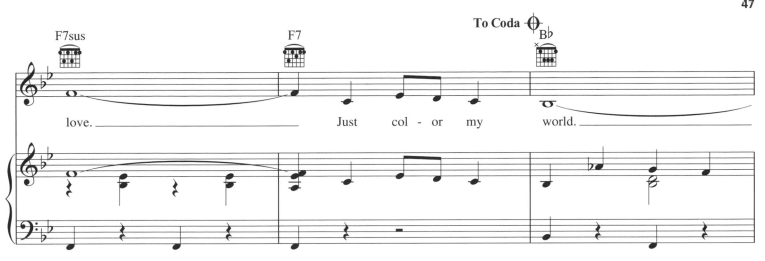

love. _____ Just col - or my world. _____

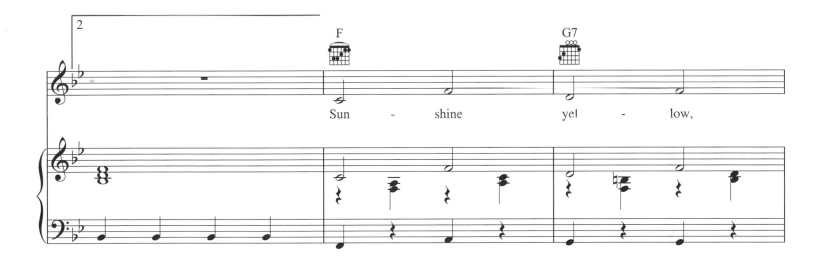

Sun - shine yel - low,

or - ange blos - som, laugh - ing

fac - es ev - 'ry - where.

D.S. al Coda

So you can

CODA

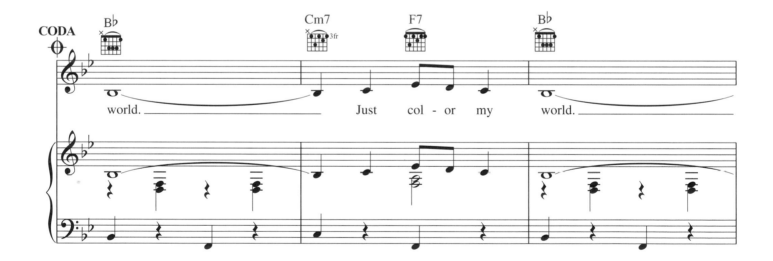

world._____ Just col - or my world._____

Just col - or my world._____

I WILL SURVIVE

Words and Music by DINO FEKARIS
and FREDERICK J. PERREN

back ___ from out-er space. I just walk in to find you here with that sad
me, ___ some-bod-y new, I'm not that chained up lit-tle per-son still in

look up-on your face. I should have changed that stu-pid lock, I should have made you leave your key, if I'd-'ve
love with you. And so you felt like drop-pin' in and just ex-pect me to be free. Well now, I'm

known for just one sec-ond you'd be back to both-er me. Go on, now } go, ___ walk out the
sav-in' all my lov-in' for some-one who's lov-in' me. Go on, now }

door; ___ just turn a-round, now, 'cause you're not wel-come an-y-more.

A FINE ROMANCE

from SWING TIME

Words by DOROTHY FIELDS
Music by JEROME KERN

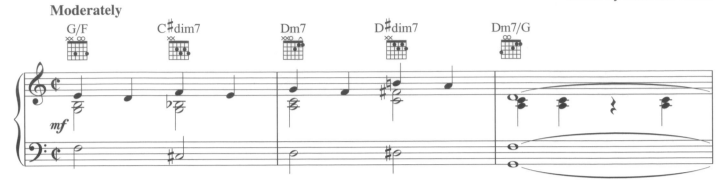

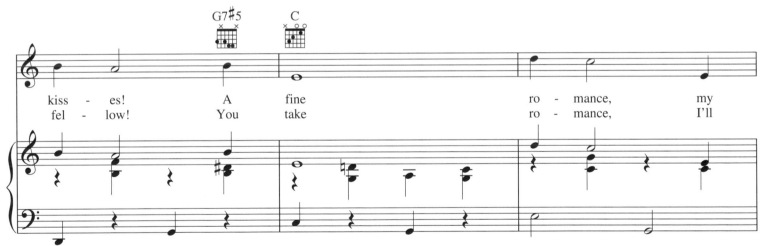

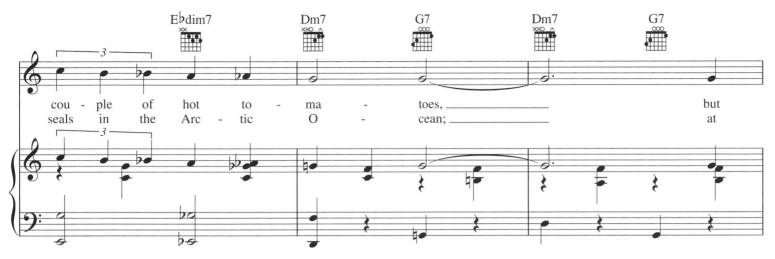

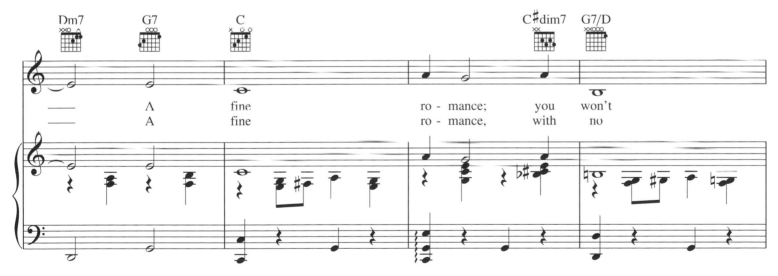

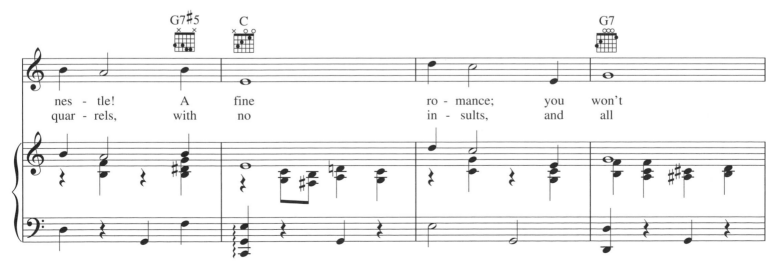

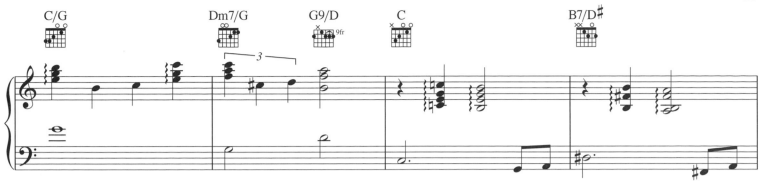

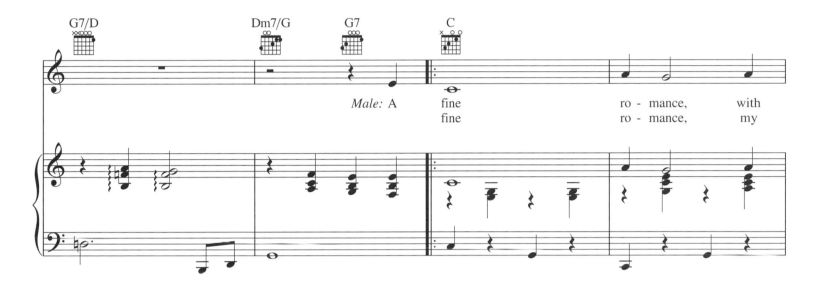

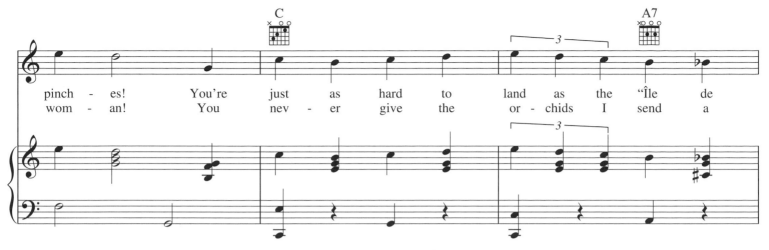

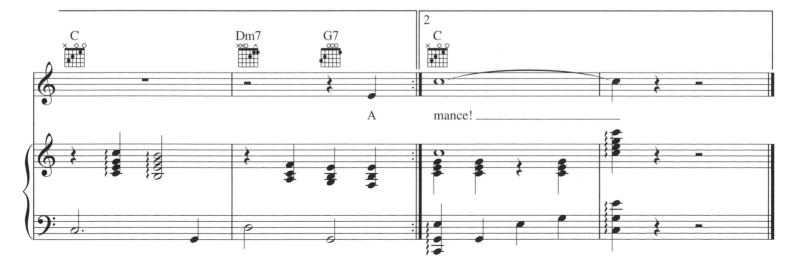

SHAKE YOUR GROOVE THING

Words and Music by DINO FEKARIS
and FREDDIE PERREN

Bright, with a steady beat

Opt. 8vb throughout

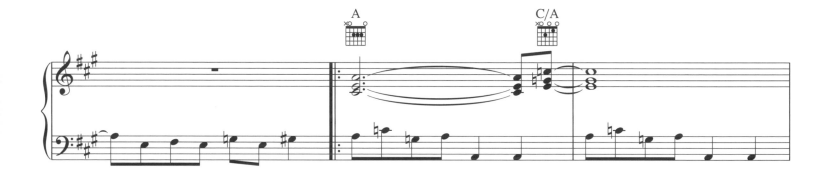

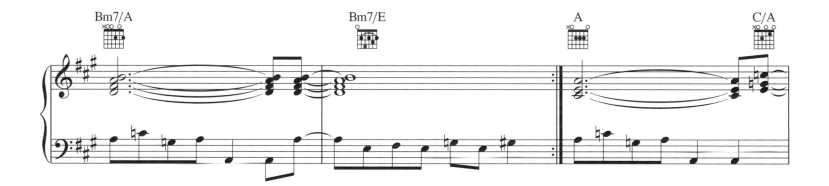

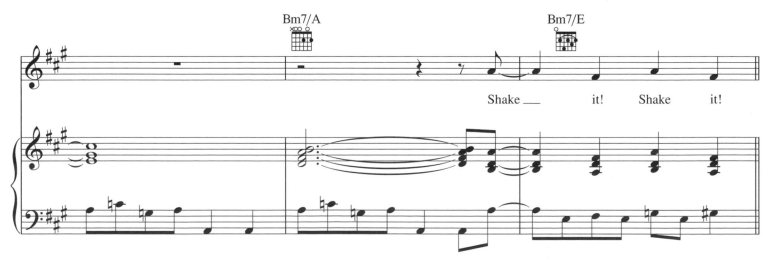

Shake ___ it! Shake it!

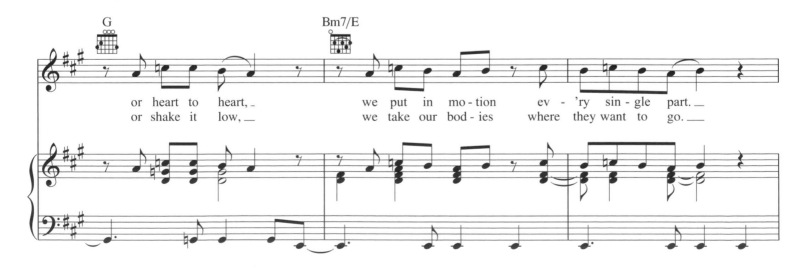

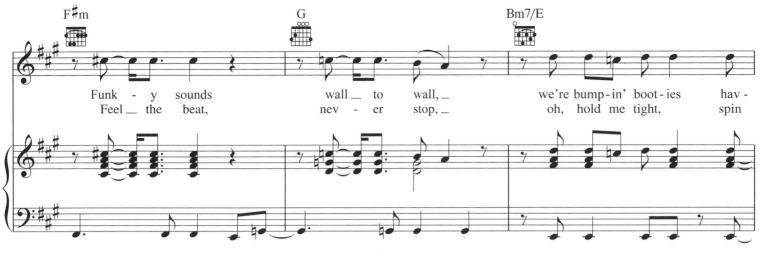

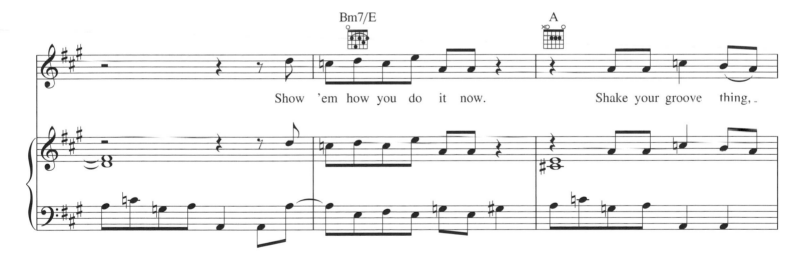

D.S. al Coda

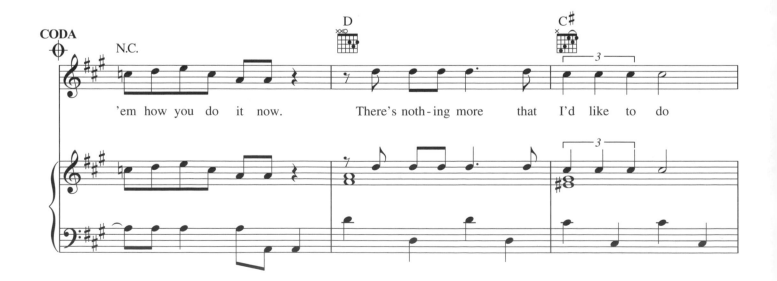

'em how you do it now.   There's noth-ing more   that   I'd like to do

we put in mo-tion ev-'ry sin-gle part. ___ Funk - y sounds

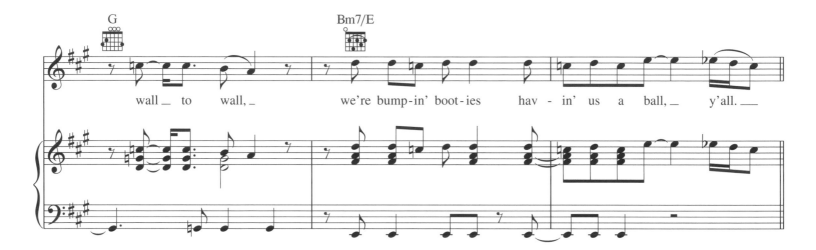

wall ___ to wall, ___ we're bump-in' boot-ies hav - in' us a ball, ___ y'all. ___

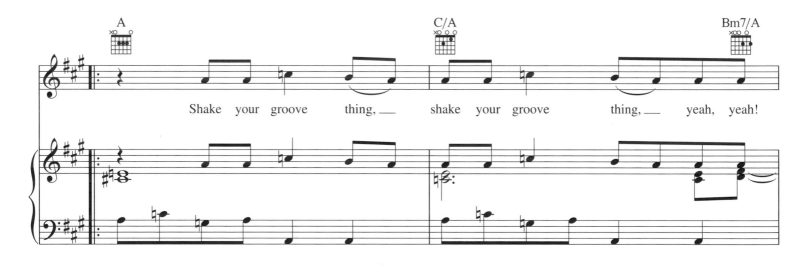

Shake your groove thing, ___ shake your groove thing, ___ yeah, yeah!

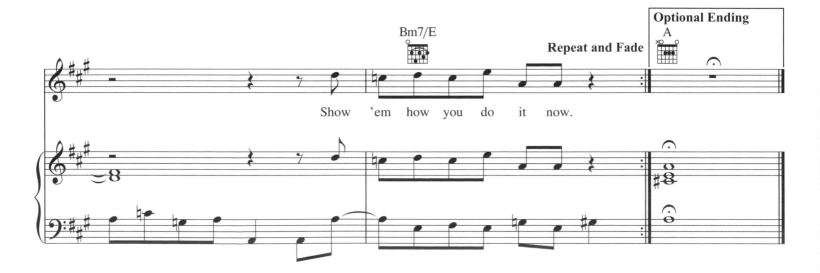

Show 'em how you do it now.

POP MUZIK

Words and Music by
ROBIN EDMOND SCOTT

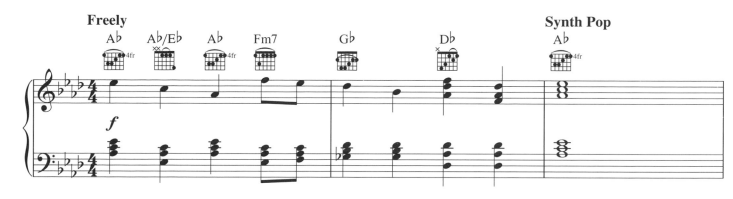

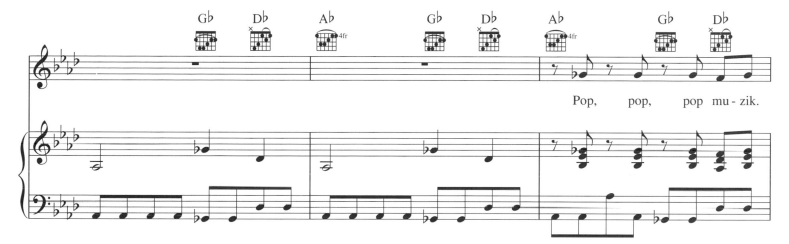

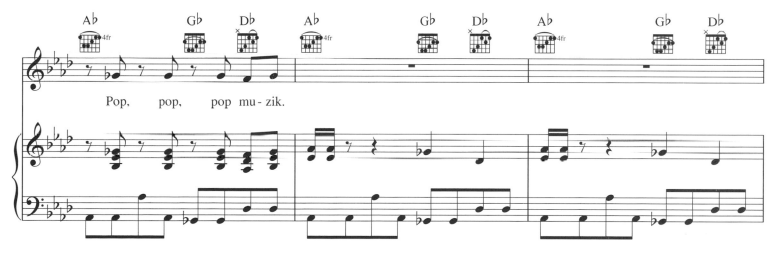

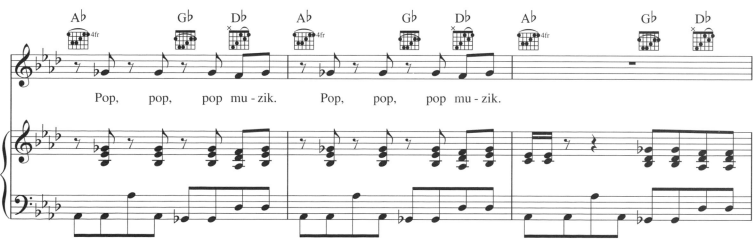

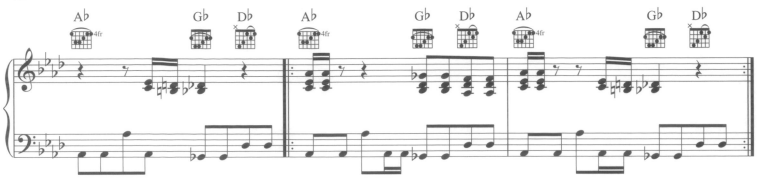

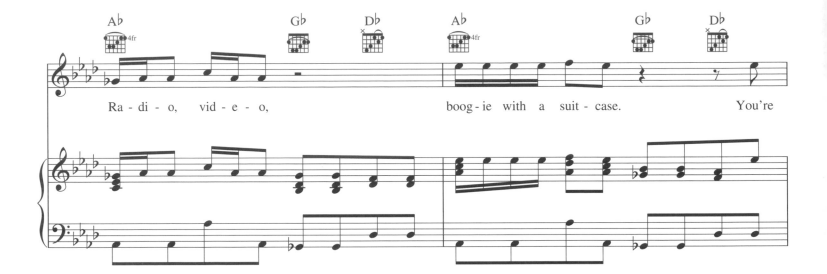

Ra - di - o, vid - e - o, boog - ie with a suit - case. You're

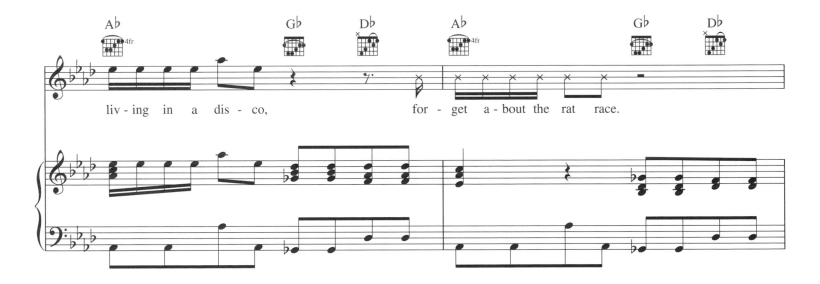

liv - ing in a dis - co, for - get a - bout the rat race.

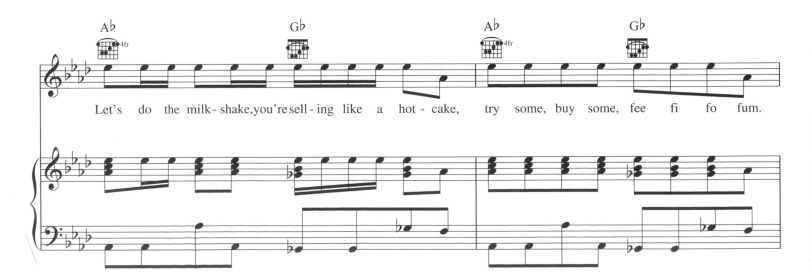

Let's do the milk - shake, you're sell - ing like a hot - cake, try some, buy some, fee fi fo fum.

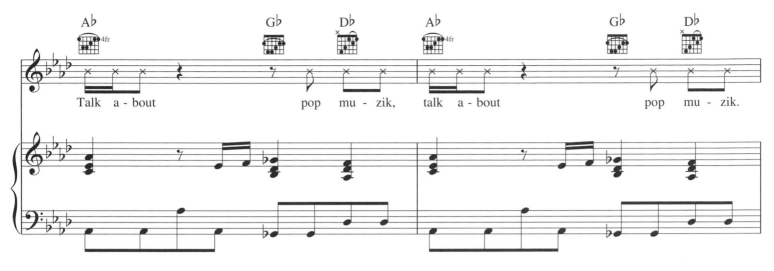

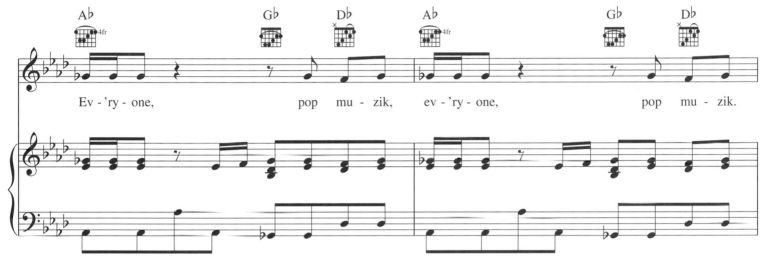

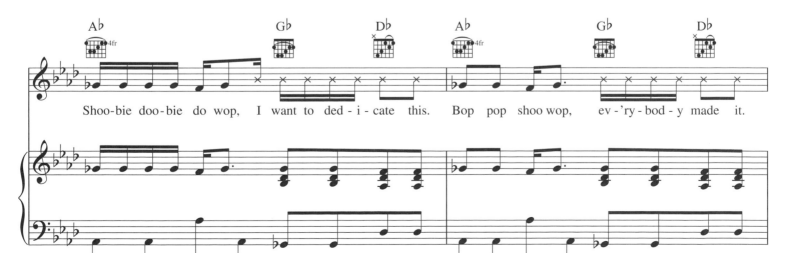

Shoo-bie doo-bie do wop, in-fil-trate it. Bop pop shoo wop, ac-ti-vate it.

New York, Lon-don, Par-is, Mu-nich, ev-'ry-bod-y talk a-bout pop mu-zik.

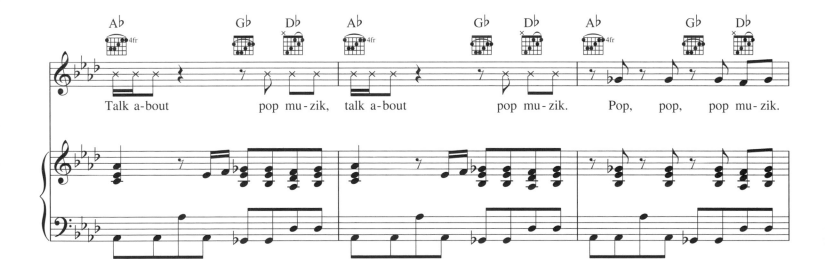

Talk a-bout pop mu-zik, talk a-bout pop mu-zik. Pop, pop, pop mu-zik.

Pop, pop, pop mu-zik. Sing it in the sub-way,
Dance in the su-per-mart,

Bop pop shoo wop, me, me, me, me. Shoo-bie doo-bie do wop, right in - be-tween - ie.
Bop pop shoo wop, they want to sur - round _ you. Shoo-bie doo-bie do wop, it's all a - round you.

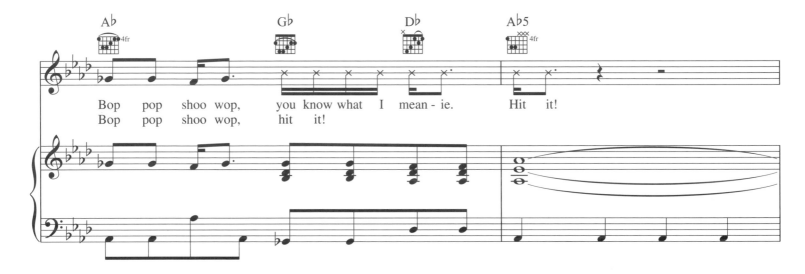

Bop pop shoo wop, you know what I mean - ie. Hit it!
Bop pop shoo wop, hit it!

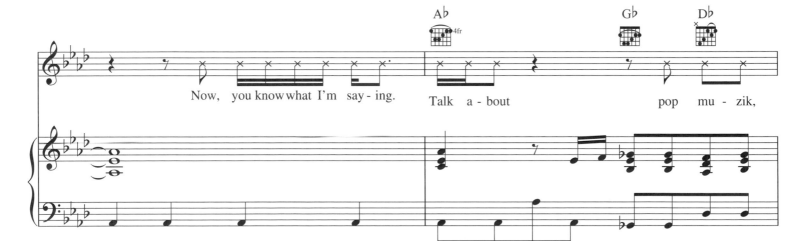

Now, you know what I'm say - ing. Talk a - bout pop mu - zik,

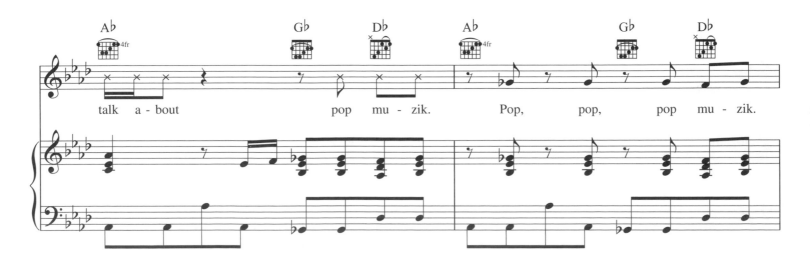

talk a - bout pop mu - zik. Pop, pop, pop mu - zik.

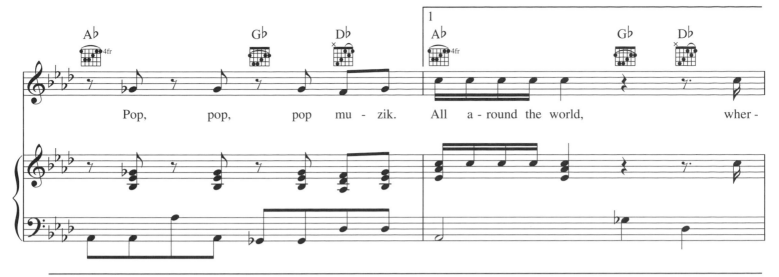

Pop, pop, pop mu - zik. All a - round the world, wher -

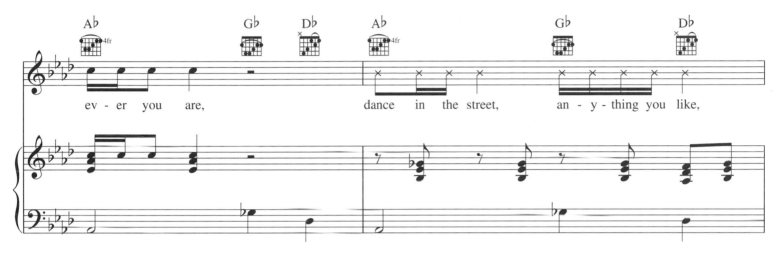

ev - er you are, dance in the street, an - y - thing you like,

do it in your car in the mid-dle of the night. La la la la la la la la la la la

la la la la la. La la la la la la la la la la la la la la la la

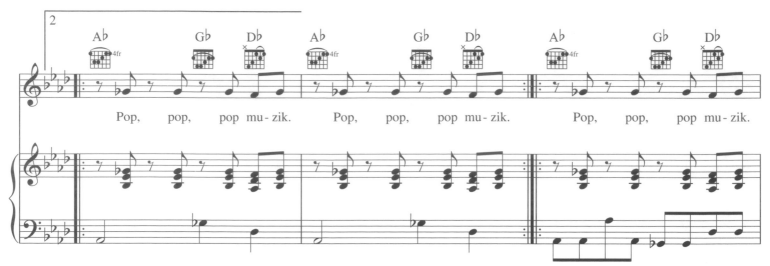

Pop, pop, pop mu-zik. Pop, pop, pop mu-zik. Pop, pop, pop mu-zik.

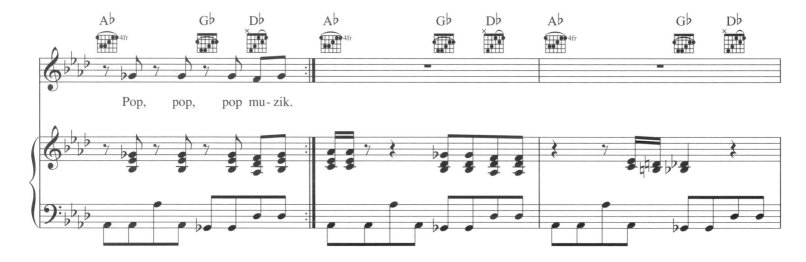

Pop, pop, pop mu-zik.

New York, Lon - don, Par - is, Mu - nich, ev-'ry-bod - y talk a - bout pop mu-zik.

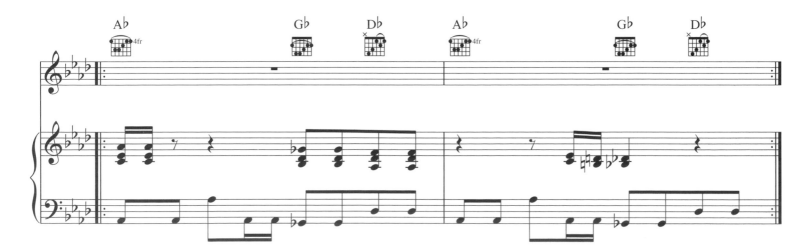

Shoo-bie doo-bie do wop,   Bop pop shoo wop,

New York, Lon-don, Par - is, Mu - nich, ev-'ry-bod-y talk a-bout pop mu - zik.

Talk a-bout   pop mu-zik, talk a bout   pop mu-zik. Pop, pop, pop mu-zik.

Pop, pop, pop mu-zik.

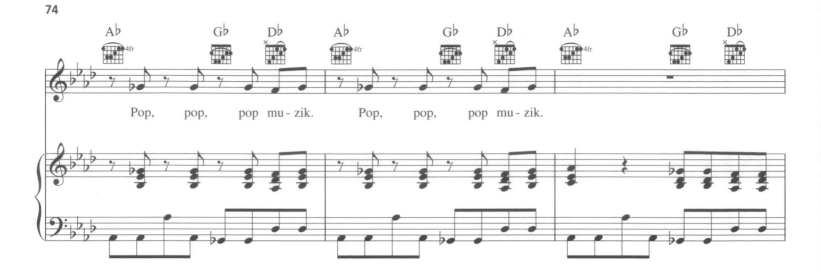

Pop, pop, pop mu-zik. Pop, pop, pop mu-zik.

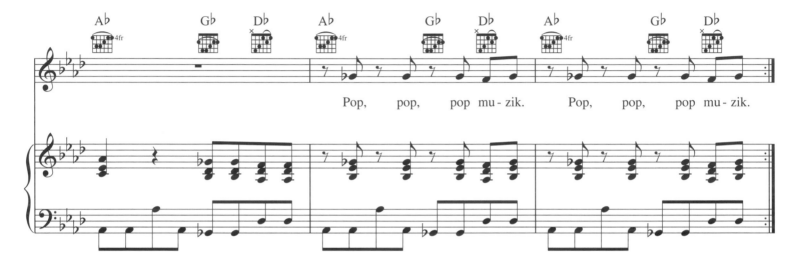

Pop, pop, pop mu-zik. Pop, pop, pop mu-zik.

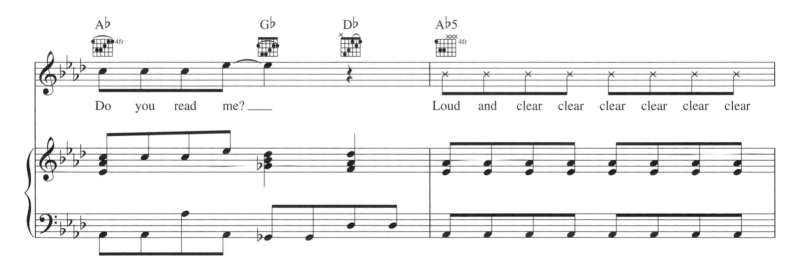

Do you read me? ___ Loud and clear clear clear clear clear clear

clear clear clear clear clear clear clear clear clear clear clear clear.

GIRLS JUST WANT TO HAVE FUN

Words and Music by
ROBERT HAZARD

I come home in the morn-ing light.__ My moth-
The phone rings in the mid-dle of the night. My fa-
Some boys take a beau-ti-ful girl__ and hide__

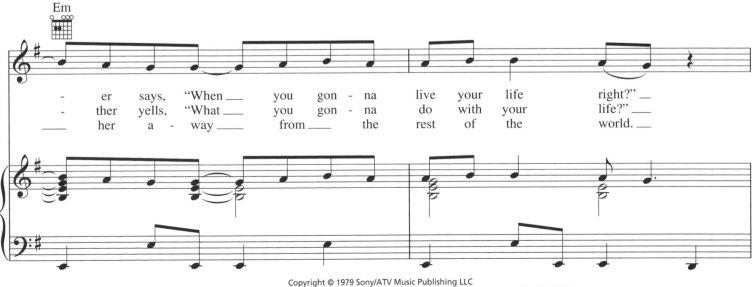

-er says, "When__ you gon-na live your life right?"__
-ther yells, "What__ you gon-na do with your life?"__
__her a-way__ from__ the rest of the world.__

Oh, Moth-er dear, __ we're not the for - tu - nate ones. And
Oh, Dad - dy dear, __ you know you're still num - ber one. But
I want to be __ the one to walk in __ the sun. Oh,

girls,
girls, they want to have fu - un. Oh, __ girls just want to have
girls,

fun. __

girls just want to have... That's all they real - ly want: __

some fun.

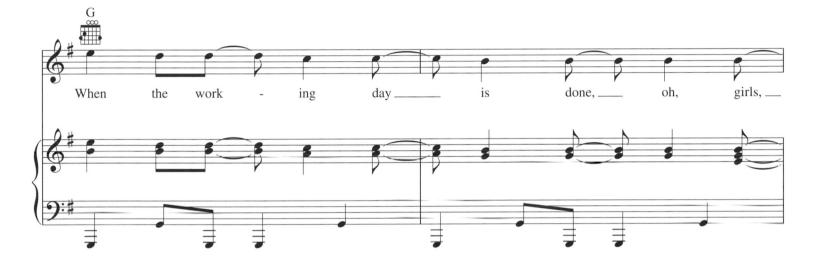

When the work - ing day _____ is done, _____ oh, girls, _____

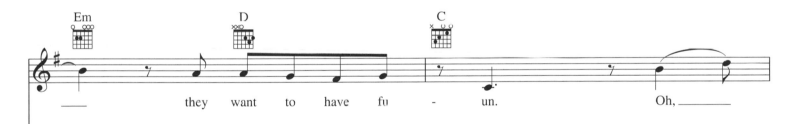

_____ they want to have fu - un. Oh, _____

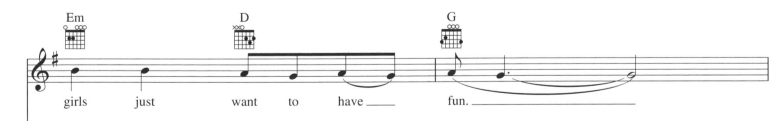

girls just want to have _____ fun. _____

HOT STUFF

Words and Music by PETE BELLOTTE,
HAROLD FALTERMEIER and KEITH FORSEY

Moderate Disco

Sit-tin' here ___ eat-in' my heart ___ out wait-in',
Look-in' for a lov-er who needs ___ an-oth-er, don't

wait-in' for some lov-er to call.
want an-oth-er night on my own. ___

Dialed a-bout a thou-sand num-
Wan-na share my love with a warm-

-bers late-ly,
-blood-ed lov-er;

al-most rang the phone off the wall. ___
wan-na bring a wild man back home.

Look-in' got some
Got-ta have some

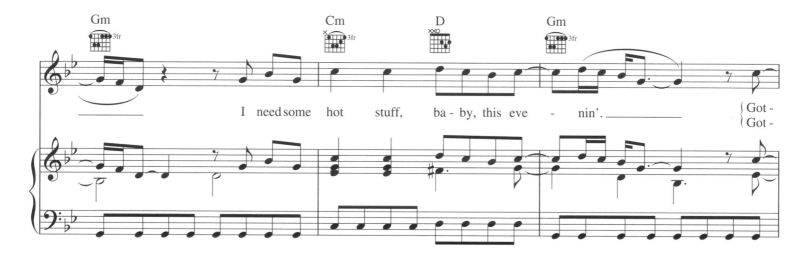

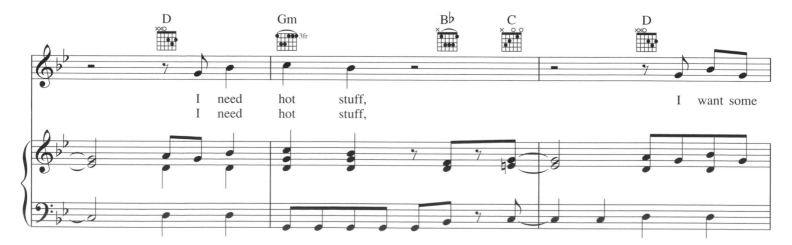

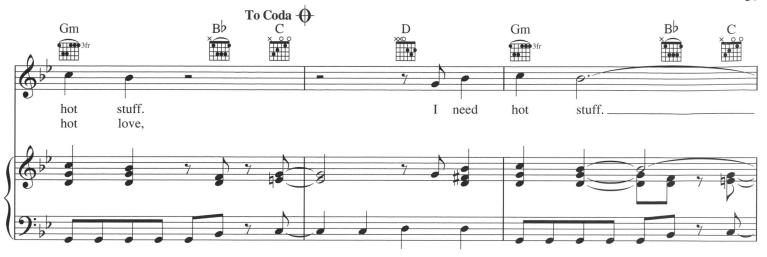

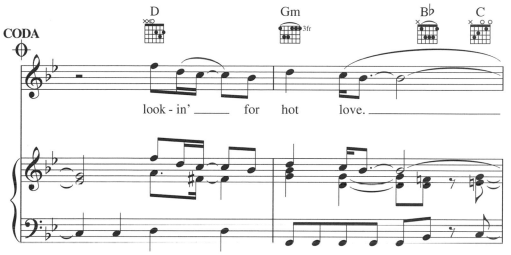

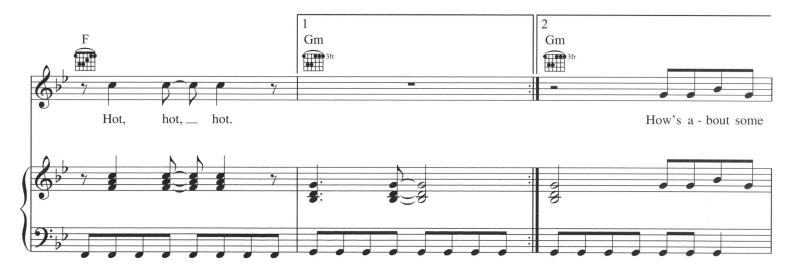

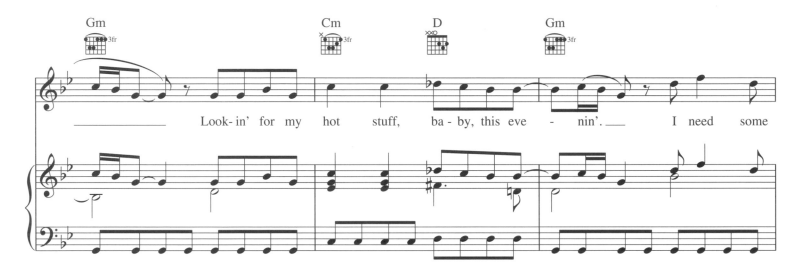

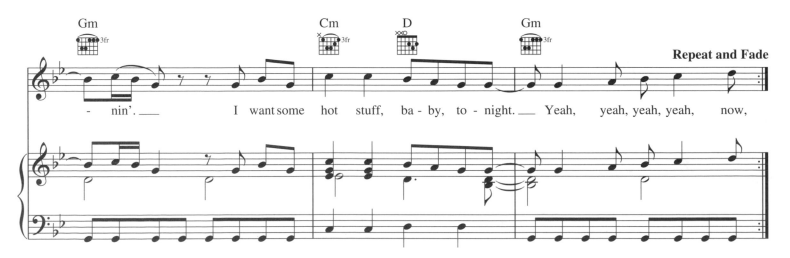

MacARTHUR PARK

Words and Music by
JIMMY WEBB

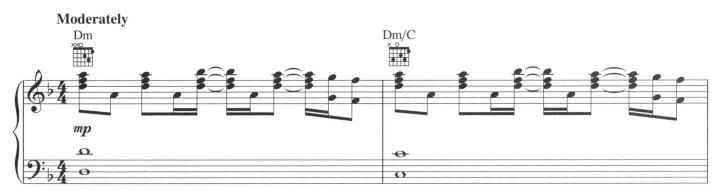

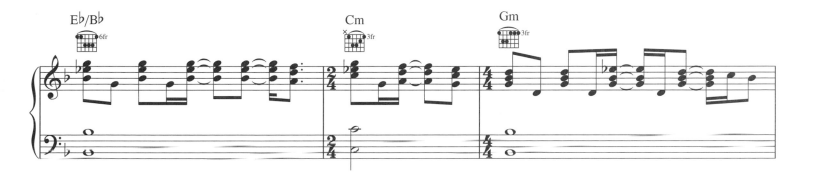

Spring was nev-er wait-ing _____ for us, girl, it ran _____ one _____ step a-
I re-call the yel-low cot-ton dress foam-ing like a

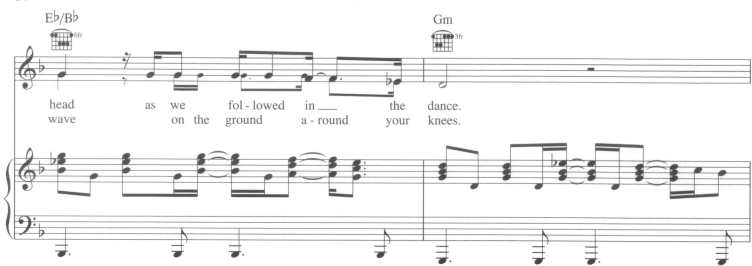

84

head as we fol-lowed in ___ the dance.
wave on the ground a-round your knees.

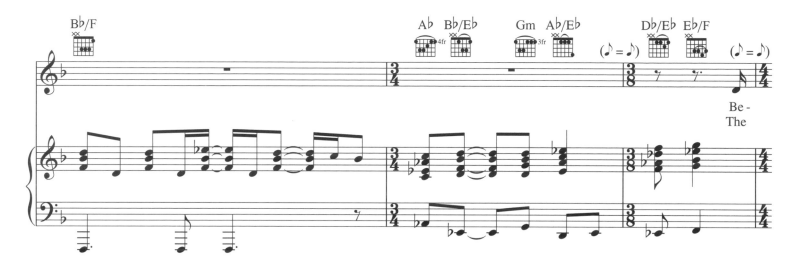

Be-
The

tween the part-ed pag - es ___ and were pressed in love's ___ hot fe-vered i -
birds like ten-der ba - bies ___ in your hands and the old man play-ing cheq -

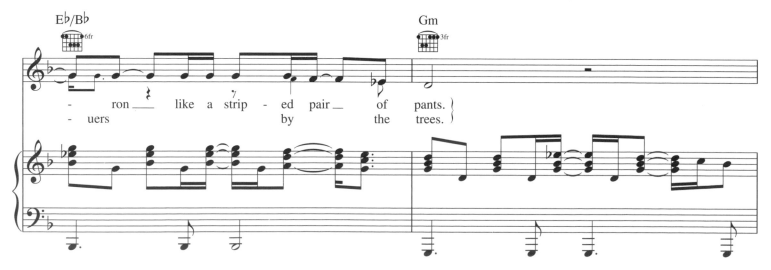

- ron ___ like a strip - ed pair ___ of pants.
- uers by the trees.

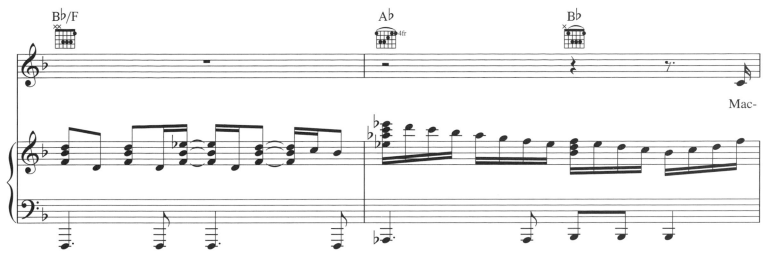

Mac-

Ar - thur's Park is melt - ing in the dark, ___ all the sweet green ic - ing

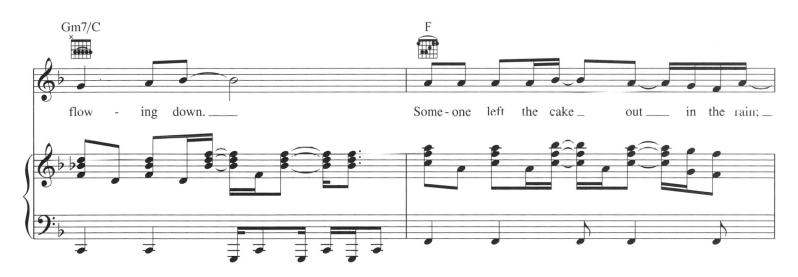

flow - ing down. ___ Some - one left the cake ___ out ___ in the rain; ___

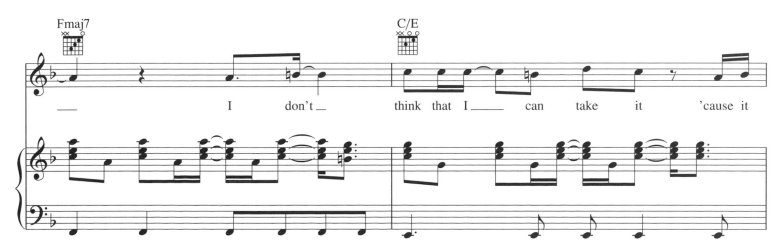

___ I don't ___ think that I ___ can take it 'cause it

took so long to bake __ it and I'll nev-er have __ that rec-i-pe __ a-

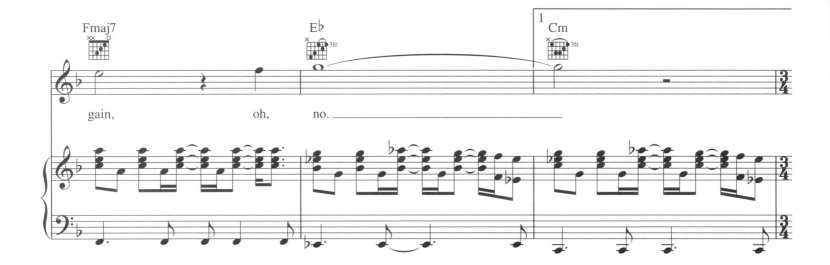

gain, oh, no. _____

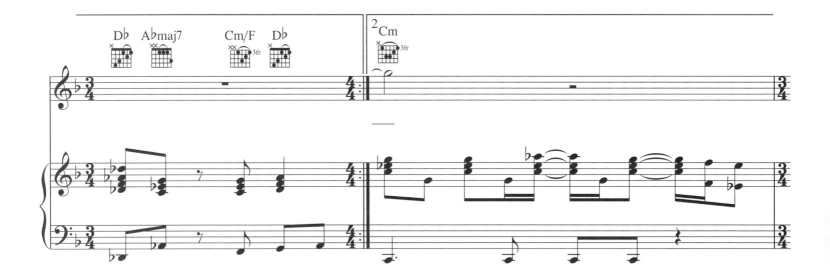

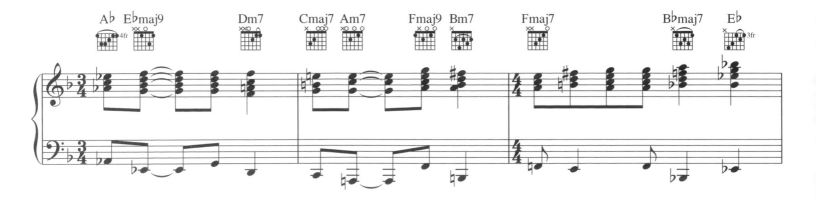

There will be an-oth-er song _ for

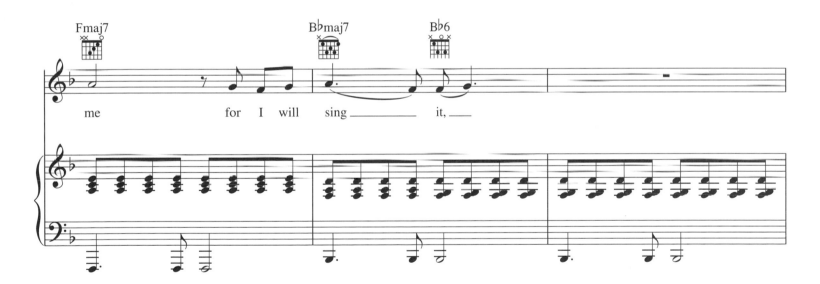

me   for I will sing _____ it, ____

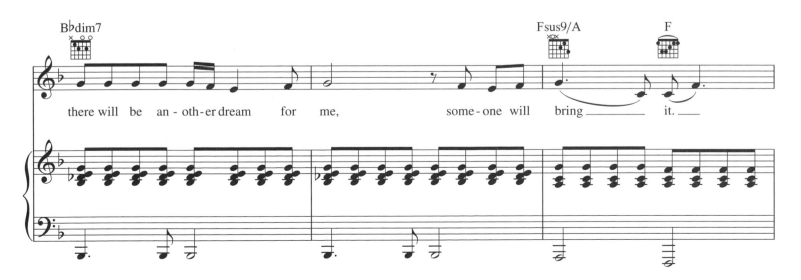

there will be an-oth-er dream _ for me,   some-one will bring _____ it. ____

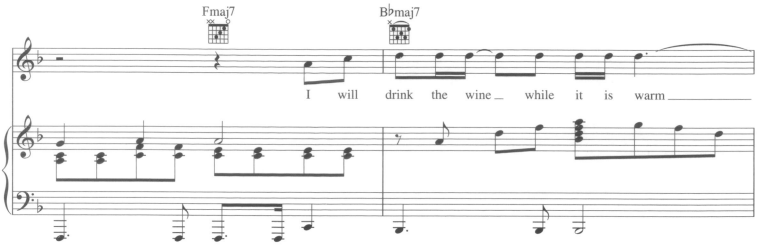

I will drink the wine ___ while it is warm ___

___ and nev - er let ___ you catch ___ me look - ing at the sun, ___

and af - ter all the loves ___ of my life,

af - ter all the loves ___ of my life ___ you'll ___ still be the one.

I will take my life _____ in - to my hands _____ and I will

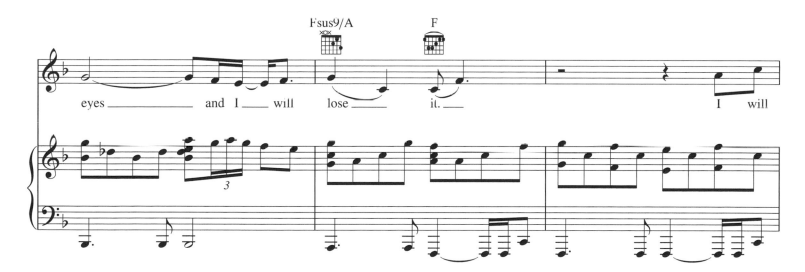

use _____ it. ___ I will win the wor - ship ___ in their

eyes _____ and I ___ will lose _____ it. ___ I will

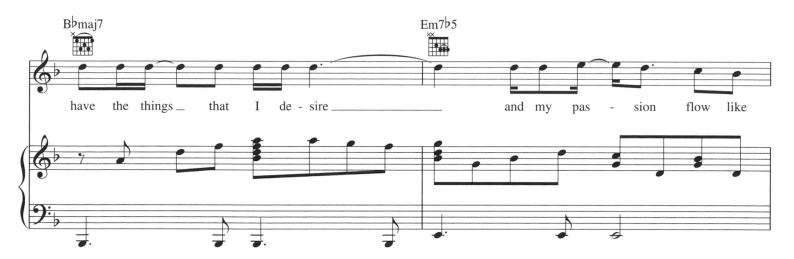

have the things ___ that I de - sire _____ and my pas - sion flow like

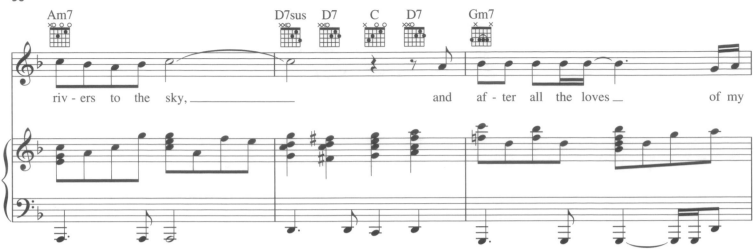

riv - ers to the sky, _____ and af - ter all the loves ___ of my

life, oh, af - ter all the loves ___ of my life I'll be think-ing of

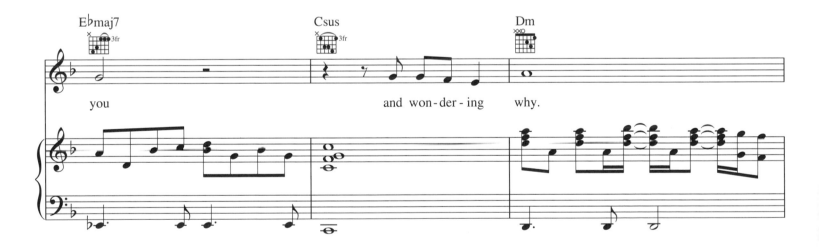

you and won-der-ing why.

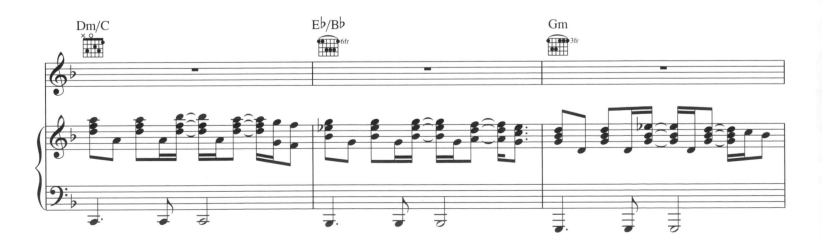

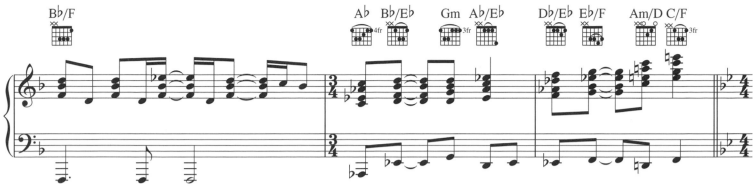

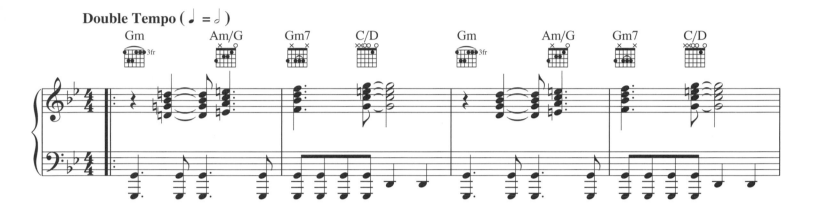

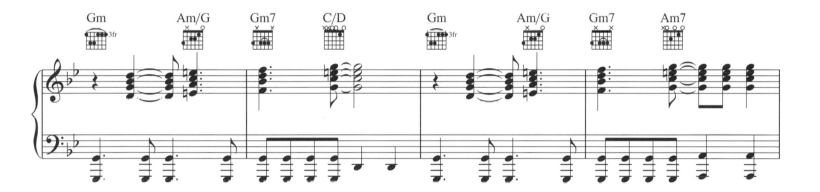

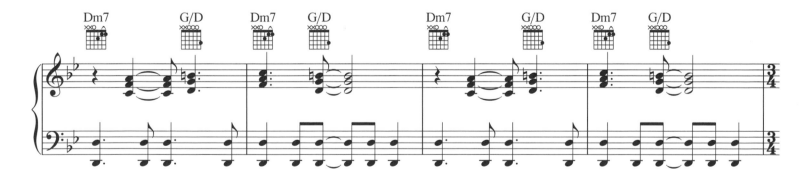

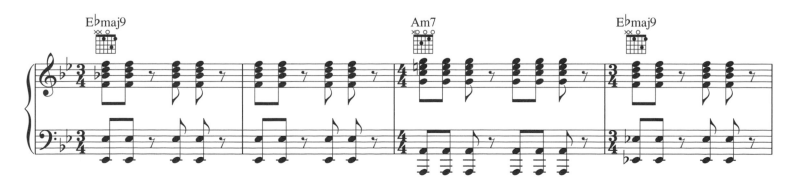

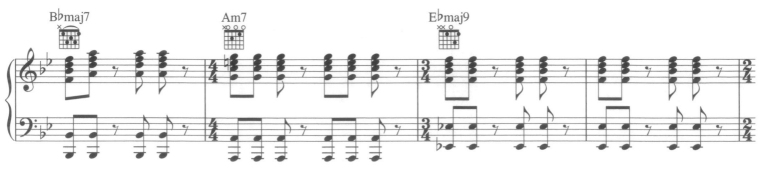

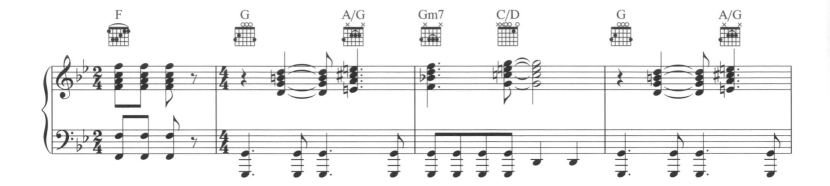

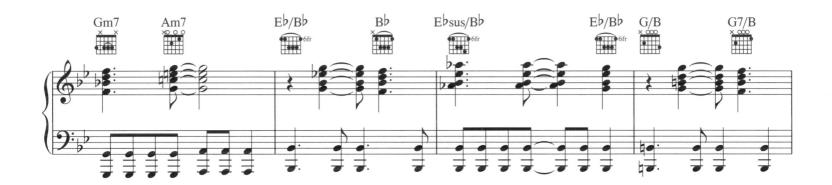

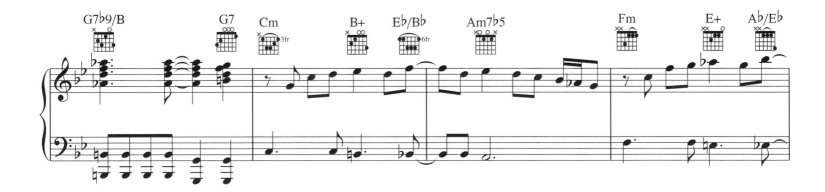

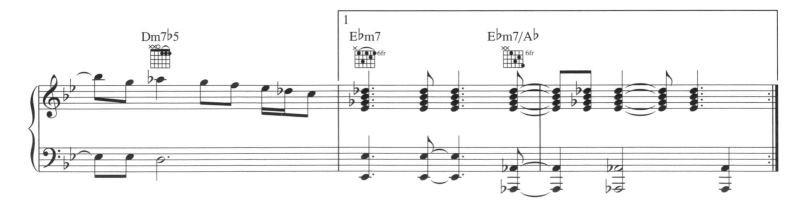

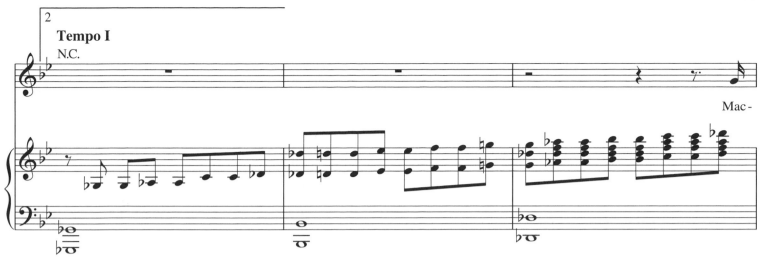

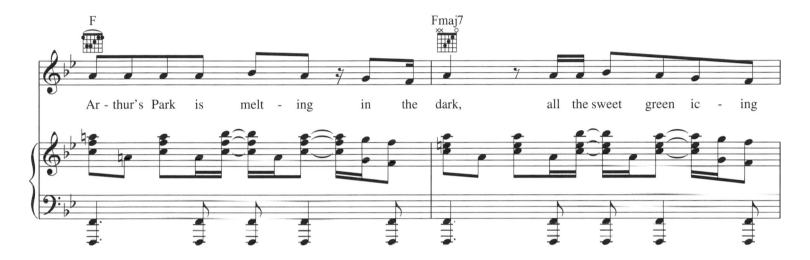

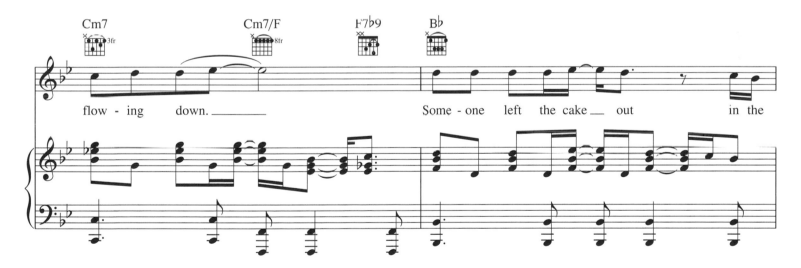

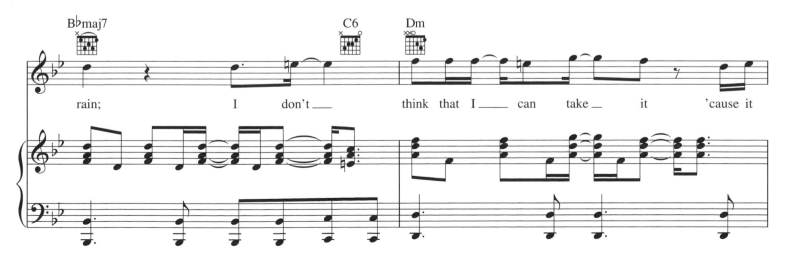

took so long to bake it and I'll nev-er have that rec-i-pe a-

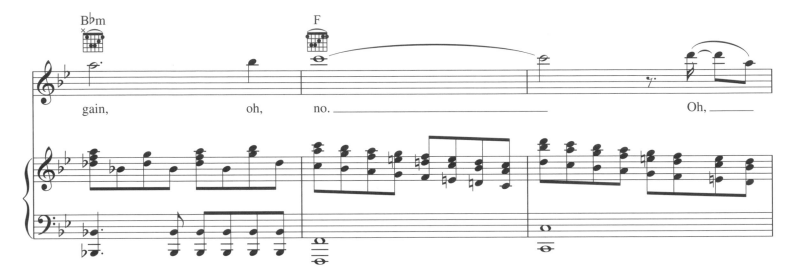

gain, oh, no. _____ Oh, _____

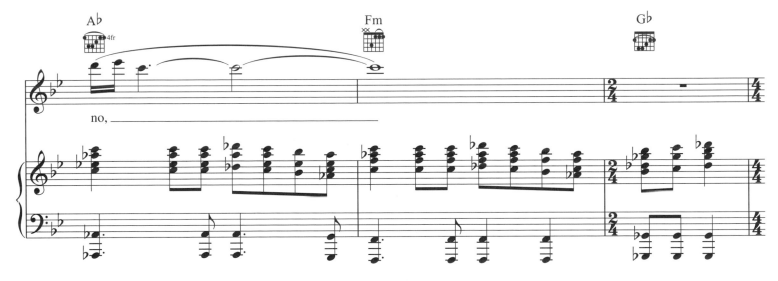

no, _____

no, no, no, oh, no. _____

ALWAYS ON MY MIND

Words and Music by WAYNE THOMPSON,
MARK JAMES and JOHNNY CHRISTOPHER

me, give me one more chance to keep you sat-is-fied, sat-is-

D.S. al Coda

fied.

CODA

You are al-ways on my

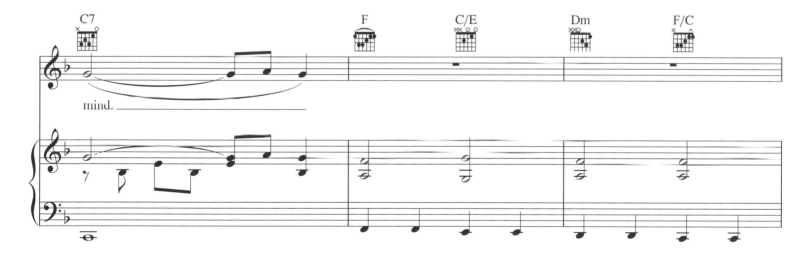

mind.

You are al-ways on my mind.

rit.

LIKE A PRAYER

Words and Music by PATRICK LEONARD
and MADONNA CICCONE

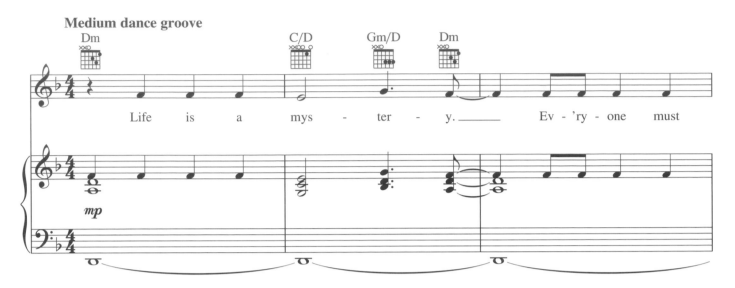

Life is a mys - ter - y. _____ Ev - 'ry - one must

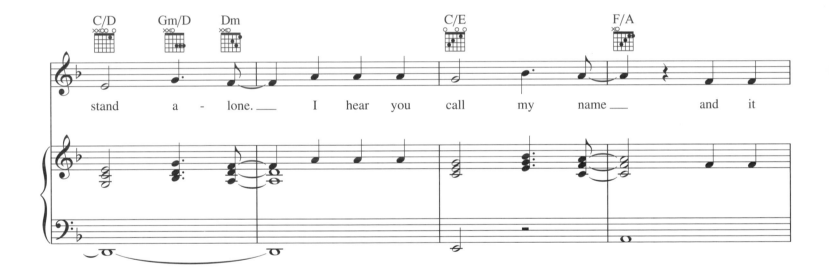

stand a - lone. ___ I hear you call my name ___ and it

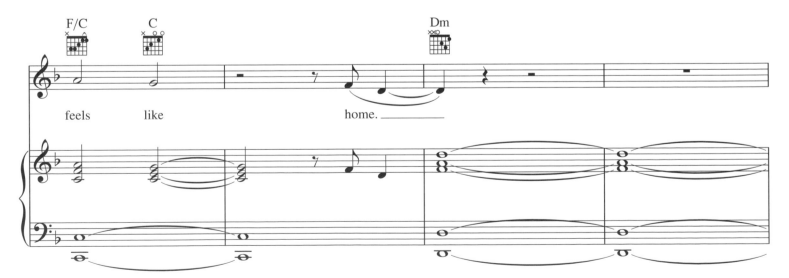

feels like home. _____

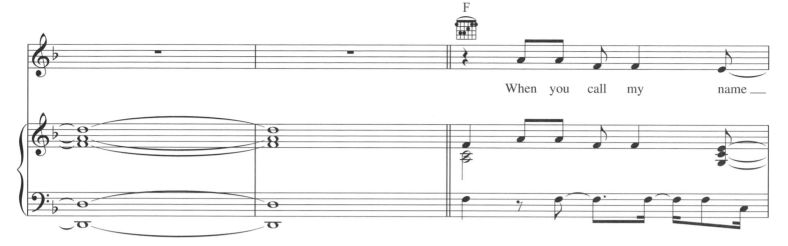

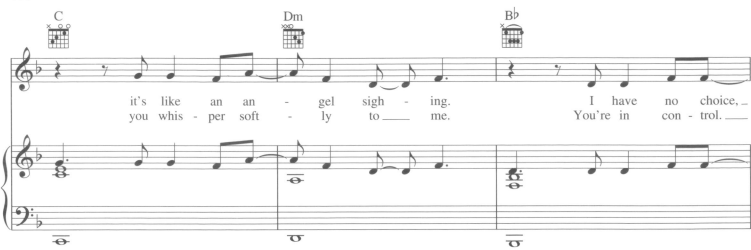

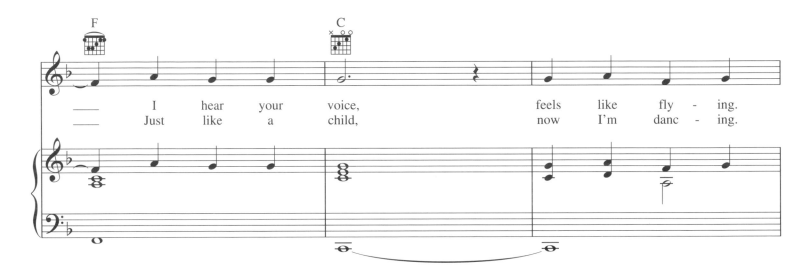

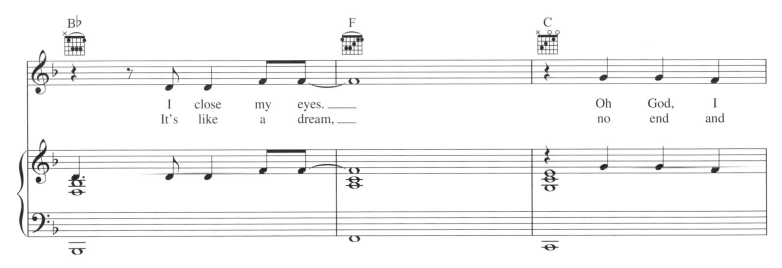

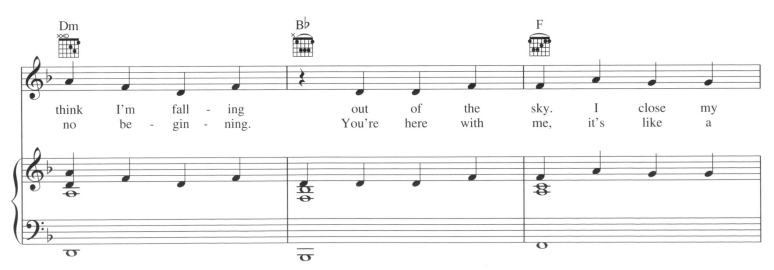

eyes.

dream.

Heav - en help me.

Let the help choir sing.

When you call my ____ name ____

____ it's like a lit - tle ____ prayer. ____ I'm down on my ____ knees, ____ I wan-na take you

there. In the mid - night hour ____ I can feel ____ your pow - er just like a ____ prayer. ____

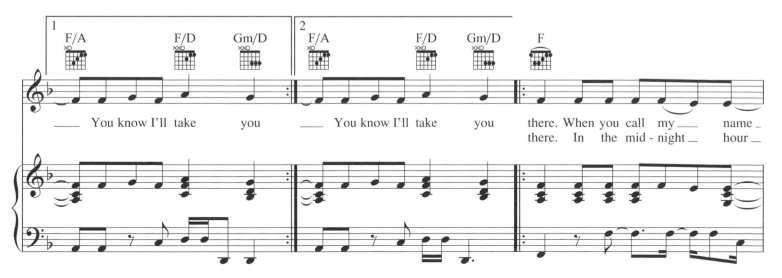

1. ____ You know I'll take you

2. ____ You know I'll take you there. When you call my ____ name ____

there. In the mid - night ____ hour ____

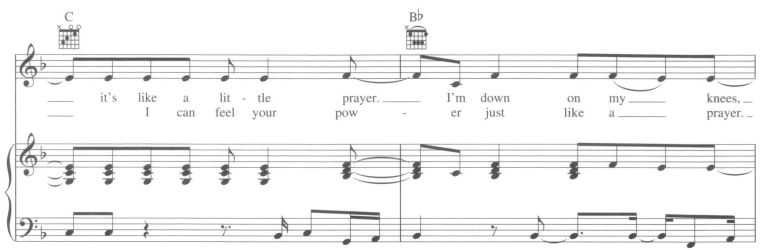

it's like a lit - tle prayer. _____ I'm down on my _____ knees,
I can feel your pow - er just on like a _____ prayer. _

_____ I wan - na take you
_____ You know I'll take you there.

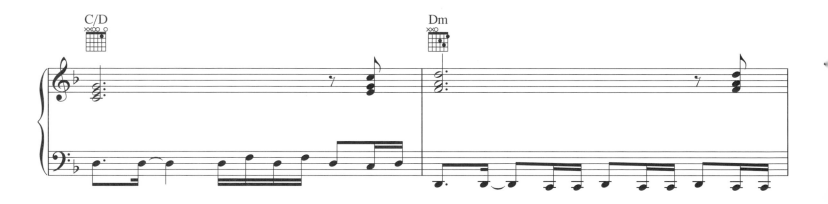

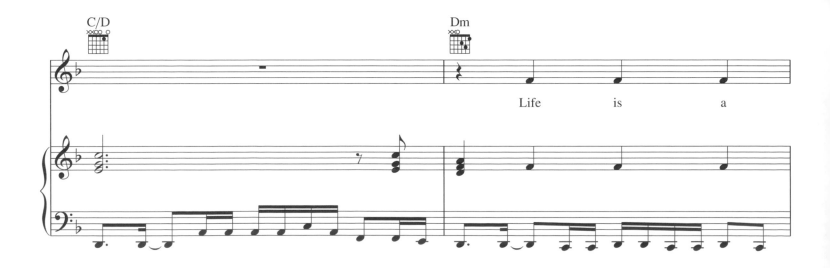

Life is a

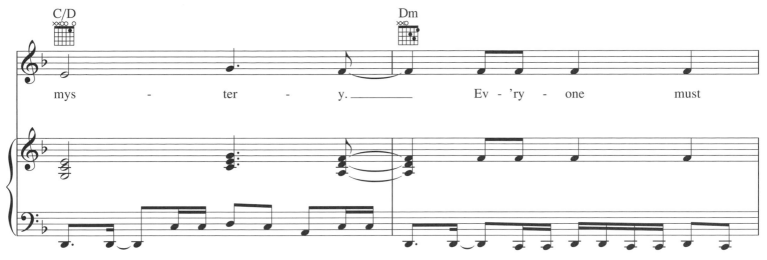

mys - ter - y. _____ Ev - 'ry - one must

stand a - lone. _____ I hear you

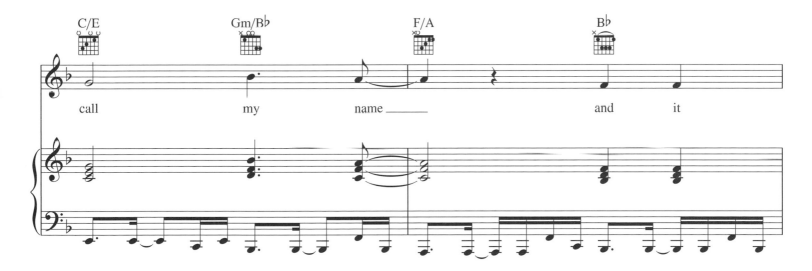

call my name _____ and it

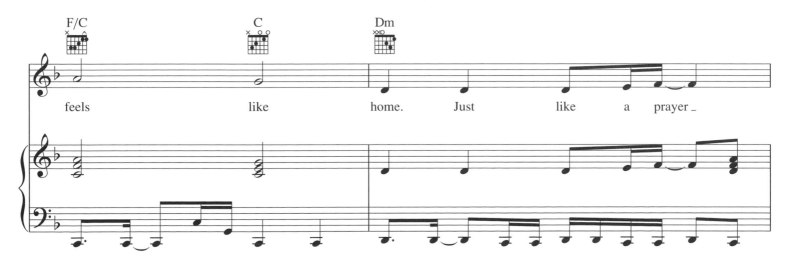

feels like home. Just like a prayer _

your voice can take me there. Just like a muse to me.

You are a mys - ter - y. Just like a dream

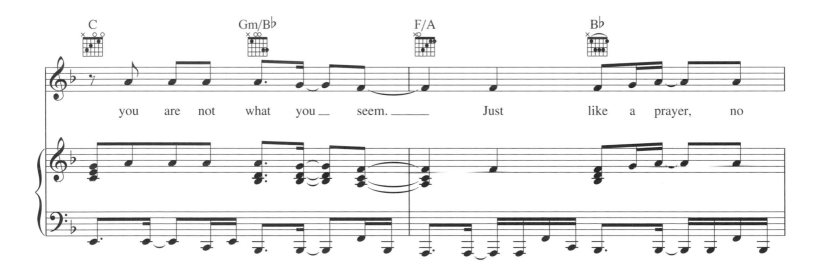

you are not what you seem. Just like a prayer, no

choice, your voice can take me there. (Just like a prayer I'll

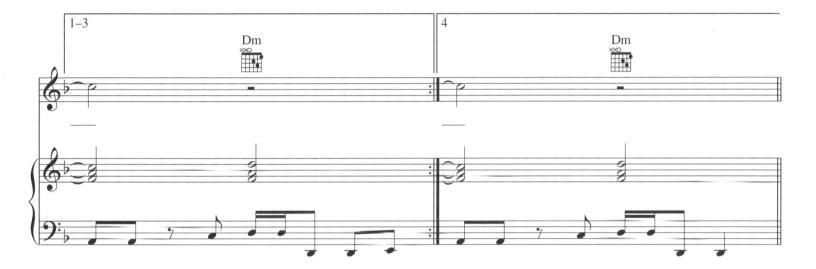

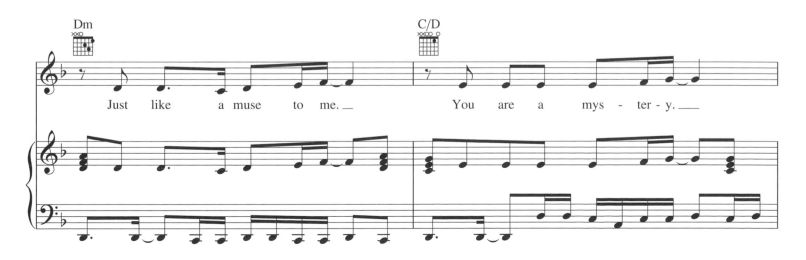

Just like a dream, _ you are not what you _ seem. _

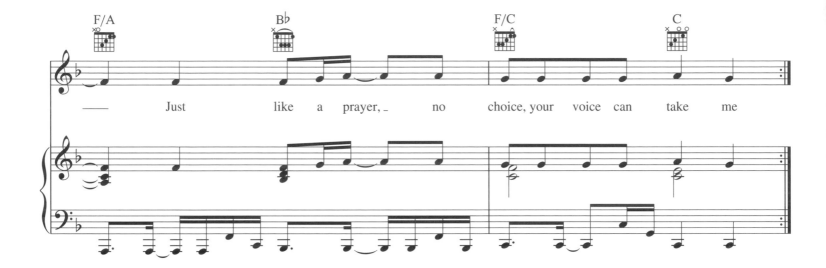

_ Just like a prayer, _ no choice, your voice can take me

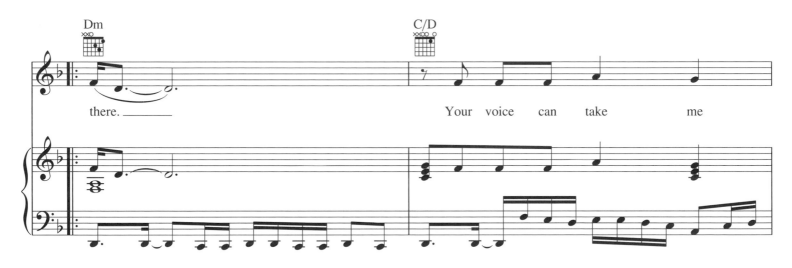

there. _____ Your voice can take me

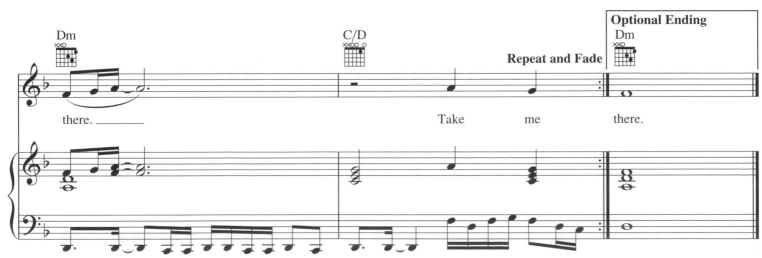

there. _____ Take me there.

WE BELONG

Words and Music by DAVID ERIC LOWEN
and DANIEL NAVARRO

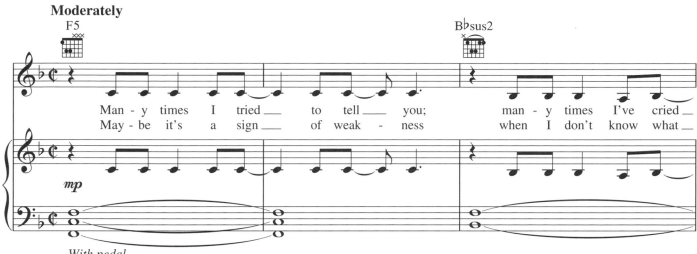

Moderately

Man-y times I tried to tell you; man-y times I've cried
May-be it's a sign of weak-ness when I don't know what

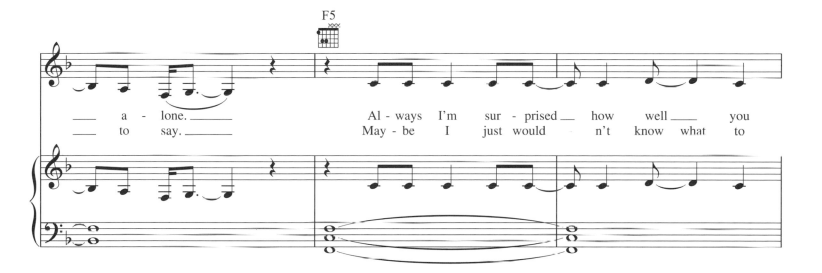

___ a - lone. ___ Al - ways I'm sur - prised how well ___ you
___ to say. ___ May - be I just would n't know what to

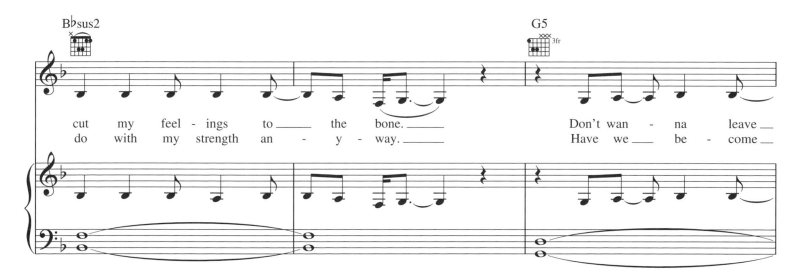

cut my feel-ings to ___ the bone. Don't wan - na leave ___
do with my strength an - y - way. ___ Have we ___ be - come ___

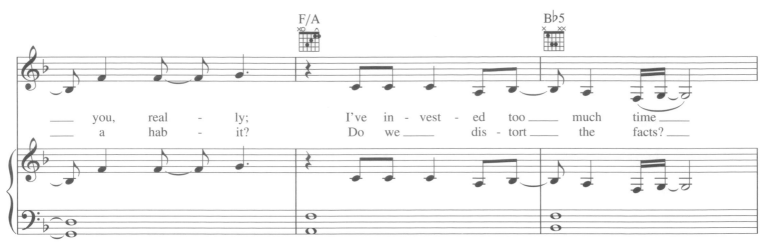

you, real - ly; I've in - vest - ed too ___ much time ___
a hab - it? Do we ___ dis - tort ___ the facts? ___

to give ___ you up ___ that eas - y to the doubts that com -
Now there's ___ no look - ing for - ward, now ___ there's no turn -

- pli - cate ___ your mind. ___ We be - long to the light, we be - long to the
- ing back ___ when you say:

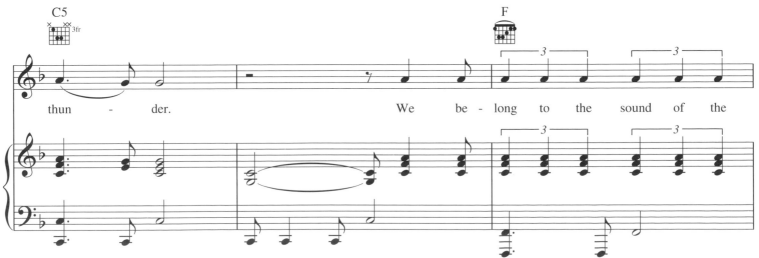

thun - der. We be - long to the sound of the

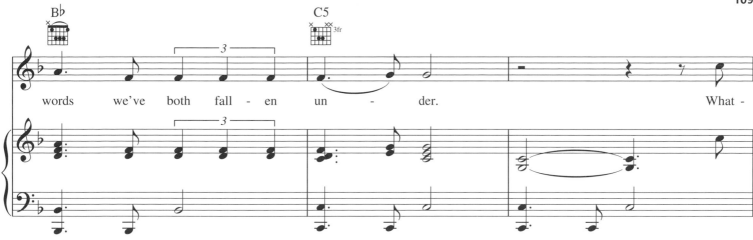

words we've both fall - en un - der. What -

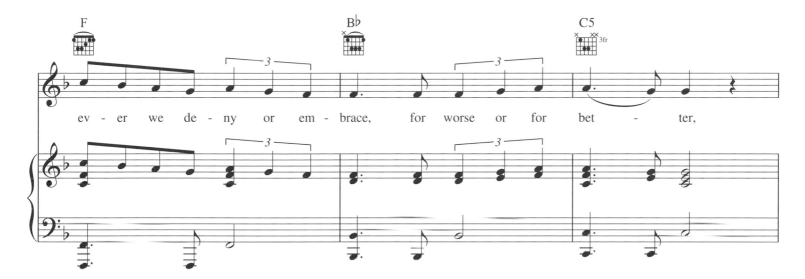

ev - er we de - ny or em - brace, for worse or for bet - ter,

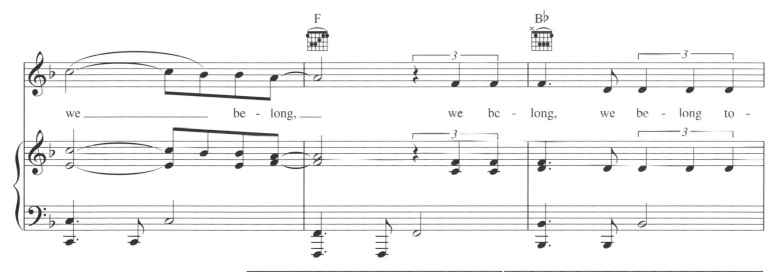

we ___ be - long, ___ we be - long, we be - long to -

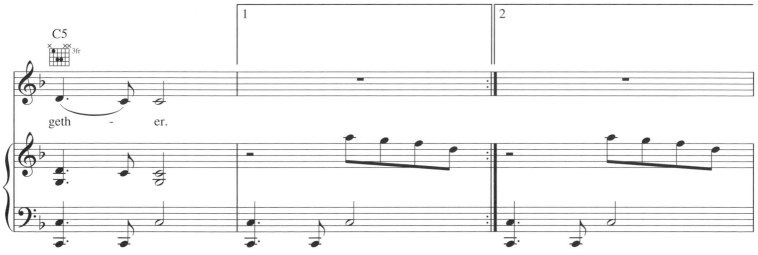

geth - er.

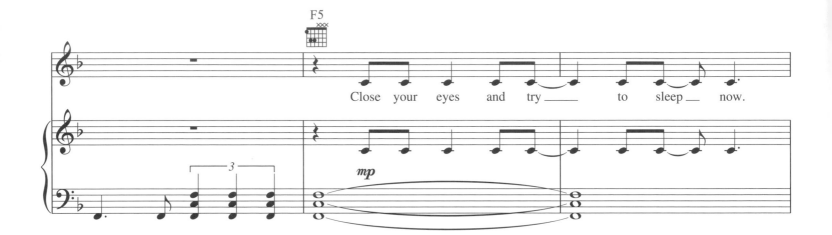

We can't_ be - gin __ to know_ it, how much_ we real -

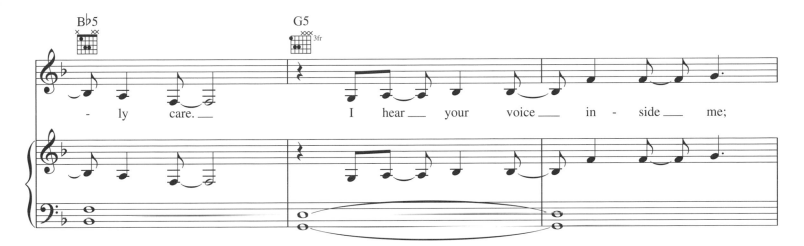

- ly care._ I hear __ your voice __ in - side __ me;

I see your face ev - 'ry - where._ Still you say:) We be - long to the

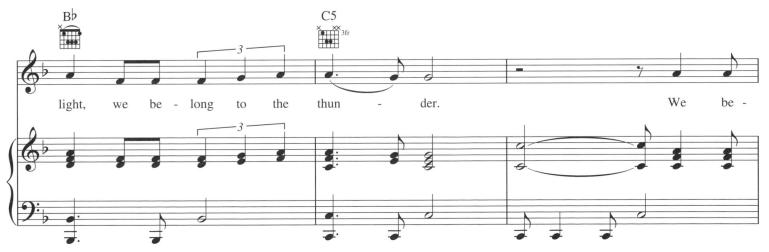

light, we be - long to the thun - der. We be -

long to the sound of the words we've both fall - en un - der.

What - ev - er we de - ny or em - brace, for worse or for

bet - ter, we ____ be - long, ____ we be -

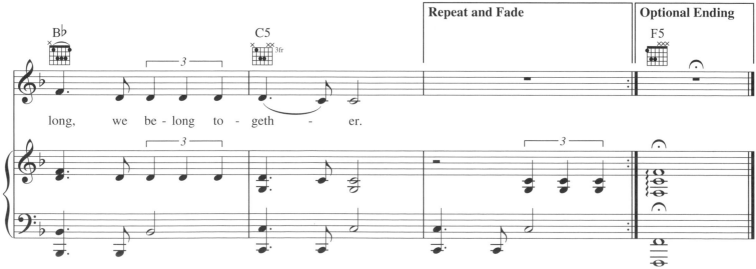

Repeat and Fade

Optional Ending

long, we be - long to - geth - er.